BULBS
for your garden

Compiled & edited by

FRANCES HUTCHISON
& JOANNE MORRIS

BayBooks

An imprint of HarperCollins*Publishers*

A Bay Books Publication

Bay Books, an imprint of
HarperCollins*Publishers*
25 Ryde Road, Pymble, Sydney, NSW 2073, Australia
31 View Road, Glenfield, Auckland 10, New Zealand

First published in Australia in 1993
Reprinted in 1993

National Library of Australia
Cataloguing-in-Publication data:

Joanne Morris.

   Bulbs for your garden.

   Includes index.
   ISBN 1 86378 038 6.

   1. Bulbs – Australia. 2. Flower gardening – Australia. I. Title.
   (Series: Bay Books gardening library).

635.944

Gardening Consultant: Frances Hutchison

Front cover photograph: Monet Tulips, supplied by Tesselaar Bulbs and Flowers
Back cover photograph: Ranunculus, Michael Cook

The publisher wishes to thank Digger's Garden Company
and Tesselaar Bulbs and Flowers for supplying
transparencies used in this book.

Printed in Australia by Griffin Press, Adelaide

8 7 6 5 4 3 2
96 95 94 93

CONTENTS

BULBS IN THE GARDEN · 4

A guide to designing your garden with bulbs, colouring your garden in each season planting bulbs in the cottage garden and the natural garden; bulbs for planting under trees, around water, for borders, beds, banks and rockeries, rooftops, terraces and paved areas, bulbs for containers, and bulbs for picking.

GROWING BULBS · 28

Basic information on types of bulbous plants, planting details, climate, soil type, fertilising, watering, lifting, growing bulbs in pots, methods of propagation, climatic problems and pests.

GROWING GUIDE · 36
Bulbs from A to Z

From Agapanthus to Zephyranthes, there is a description of each bulb, with information on cultivation and the best conditions and treatment for growing it. Planting times and flowering times are also given.

COLOURING YOUR GARDEN ALL YEAR ROUND · 88

A table for easy reference on depth of planting and distance apart, flowering and planting times and uses, of bulbs from A to Z.

LIST OF COMMON AND SCIENTIFIC NAMES · 94

DIRECTORY OF BULB NURSERIES · 96

BULBS IN THE GARDEN

Bulbs or bulbous plants can loosely be described as those plants which share the convenience of an underground food storage system. This remarkable feature means bulbs are incredibly rewarding to grow. Whether they take the form of a bulb, corm, rhizome, tuber or tuberous root they all have the ability to generously reproduce themselves at no extra cost, and when dormant require little or no attention.

This combined with the fact that there are so many beautiful varieties, available in a multitude of colours and shapes, makes bulbs a useful design tool in the garden. You can colour your garden all year round by choosing bulbs with different flowering times. Also, you can be more specific and choose water loving bulbs, shade loving bulbs, bulbs for containers — there are bulbs for all kinds of gardens and conditions.

Choosing Bulbs

Because modern hybridists have developed such a wide range of colourful, healthy and spectacular flowering plants, perhaps the most difficult task confronting the gardener is choosing the right bulbs. However, deciding what you want can be simple if you spend just a little time considering where you want to plant and the effect you hope to achieve. Fortunately, many bulb suppliers regularly issue catalogues so you can find out what bulbs are available including information as to colour, shape and height. If you know something of the country in which your bulbs originated this will also help you make your decision. Adaptable as many bulbs are, growing them in conditions similar to their native habitat will mean they are more likely to thrive. For instance *Zantedeschia* (Arum Lily) from South Africa can be expected to do well in most parts of mild temperate Australia and New Zealand while an alpine bulb from the Pyrenées will thrive better in cold Tasmania or in cooler parts of New Zealand and Britain.

It would be true to say most gardeners fondly associate bulbs with the commencement of spring. We see the first tentative snowdrop as a welcome sign that warmer weather is not far away. The early flowering spring bulbs like narcissus, tulips, hyacinths, and bluebells burst forth from

Moisture-loving Bulbs

Japanese Iris (I. ensata)
Hosta Lily
Wand Flower (Dierama)
Yellow Water Flag (Iris pseudacorus)

Shade-loving Bulbs

FULL SHADES TYPES INCLUDE:

Hymenocallis
Kaffir Lily (Clivia miniata)
Lily-of-the-valley (Convallaria majalis)
Snowflake (Leucojum)

SEMI-SHADE TYPES INCLUDE:

Bleeding Heart (Dicentra formosa)
Daffodil (Narcissus)
Glory-of-the-Snow (Chionodoxa)
Squill (Scilla)
Snowdrop (Galanthus)
Solomon's Seal (Polygonatum multiflorum)

Bulbs for Subtropical Gardens

Many bulbs work to a wet-dry cycle rather than a cool-warm one and will thrive in warmer places, particularly in shaded border situations. These include:

Achimenes
Agapanthus
Canna
Crinum
Dahlia
Freesia
Gladiolus
Lachenalia
Lilium longiflorum
Littonia
Pineapple Lily (Eucomis)
Wood Hyacinth
Zephyranthes

Bulbs for Temperate Gardens

Alliums
Anigosanthos
Amaryllis belladonna
Autumn crocus (Colchicum)
Daffodil
Dahlia*
Day Lily
Freesia*
Cape Hyacinth (Galtonia candicans)
Gladiolus*
Hippeastrum*
Lachenalia*
Snowflake (Leucojum)
Grape Hyacinth (Muscari)
Nerine*
Watsonia
(* Need to be lifted in winter)

their winter dormancy to overwhelm us with their colour and scent. But, lovely as they are, familiar cold climate bulbs like these represent only a small proportion of the many varied and easy-to-grow bulbs originating in many parts of the world. South Africa, particularly the Cape area, is host to a vast range of splendid bulbs which in all but the coldest climates can provide colour and interest in your garden all the year round. Freesias, ixia, babiana, tritonia, sparaxis, lachenalia, agapanthus, belladonna lily, gladiolus, nerine and watsonia, to name but a few, will flower in early spring, autumn or winter. The western states of North America and temperate parts of South America such as Chile and Argentina are also the homeland of a number of garden-worthy bulbs which should not be overlooked.

Right ◆ ZANTEDESCHIA (ARUM LILY) IS ONE OF THE MANY SOUTH AFRICAN BULBS WHICH GROW SUCCESSFULLY IN AUSTRALIA AND NEW ZEALAND. THEY ARE MOST EFFECTIVE PLANTED IN CLUMPS IN THE SHADE OF TREES OR CASTING REFLECTIONS IN A STILL POOL.

Left ◆ BEFORE PURCHASING YOUR BULBS, IT IS A GOOD IDEA TO WORK OUT WHERE YOU WANT TO PUT THEM AND THE COLOURS NEEDED TO GET THE BEST EFFECT. BULBS WHICH FLOWER EARLY IN SPRING WILL ENLIVEN THE GARDEN BEFORE SHRUBS AND TREES BEGIN TO DOMINATE.

Colouring Your Garden with Bulbs

Today, people are extremely conscious of the role colour can play in the garden. Perhaps Vita Sackville West's famous White Garden at Sissinghurst Castle in Kent has inspired its visitors to go out and spread the word. Ideas picked up as a result of the increasing interest in garden visiting, and the realisation that gardening can be a creative and artistic pastime for even the most amateurish of us, have also contributed to the interest in colour in the garden. Enthusiasm for Gertrude Jekyll, a painter who transferred her skills to the garden, and her magnificently orchestrated borders, has probably inspired many gardeners and landscapers.

Colour is very subjective and can be a very tricky subject but when it comes to the garden it can be even trickier. Interactions between plants often produce unexpected and surprising results. Combinations you thought might be wonderful together can be a disaster, while others that occur through chance are sometimes a triumph.

Bulbs come in such a palette of colours, you can use them like a paintbrush to 'paint' your garden. Strong colours can be used to accent those parts of the garden which require a focal point. An urn brimming with red tulips or a clump of flowering orange cliveas will immediately draw the eye to an area you wish to highlight.

RANUNCULUS COME IN A MIXED RANGE OF COLOURS WITH THE EXCEPTION OF BLUE. THEY ADD A CHEERFUL NOTE TO ANY GARDEN, AND HERE FORM A DELIGHTFUL COMBINATION WITH VIOLAS.

WHEN ORDERING TULIPS FROM CATALOGUES IT IS HELPFUL TO KNOW THEIR CLASSIFICATION

PEGGY MUNTZ

THE TUB OF RED TULIPS AT SISSINGHURST IN KENT
HAS BEEN CAREFULLY PLACED TO EMPHASISE A FOCAL
POINT IN THE GARDEN.

White is perhaps the easiest colour to handle in the garden and the most useful as it 'lifts' a shady area and glows luminously at night when other colours have faded. *Galtonia candicans* from South Africa, with its white, fragrant bell-like flowers, looks wonderful with red hot pokers *(Kniphofia)* in a sunny border. A border of black and white tulips is unusually striking.

Mixing bulbs indiscriminately is not a good idea, particularly where colour is concerned. Too many strongly contrasting colours can be a little overwhelming. Red, purple, yellow and orange are dominating colours which should be treated with care, although a 'riot' of colour may be a success in the right spot.

Some bulb growers have now made available packets of bulbs in one or a combination of colours to make your choice easier. Packets also come with single colour, in a variety of shades or combining various bulbs in one colour. When choosing your bulbs check when they flower and the conditions in which they like to grow. Bulbs which demand full sun will not be happy in semi-shade, and those which prefer moist soils won't flourish if the conditions are too dry.

Bulbs combine well with all kinds of plants. Put varieties which don't have to be lifted too often, in beds with annuals and perennials and devise interesting colour schemes of your choice. Following are some suggestions for planting bulbs to colour your garden in each season of the year.

JILL KLOSTERS

JILL KLOSTERS

WHITE WATSONIA HIGHLIGHT THE VIBRANT YELLOW OF
LABURNUM IN THIS SUPERBLY PLANTED GARDEN.

BULBS ARE THE VERY ESSENCE OF SPRING. A MASS OF
TULIPS AND BLUEBELLS OR EVEN A SINGLE DAFFODIL
CANNOT FAIL TO LIFT THE MOST FLAGGING SPIRIT IF
ONLY FOR A LITTLE WHILE.

BLUE AND WHITE FOR SPRING

A blue and white colour scheme always looks cool and restful. For the early spring flowering garden there are many white bulbs to choose from: white or creamy white *Narcissus* such as tazetta 'Paper-White' or the very handsome 'Mt Hood' daffodil, *Galanthus* (Snowdrop) for colder areas or the dainty but easier-to-grow *Leucojum* (Spring Snowflake). Elegant lily flowered white tulips or the wavy-petalled 'white parrot' tulip, White Dutch Iris and taller growing *Camassia* will all flower at about the same time as vivid blue hyacinths, *Muscari* (Grape Hyacinth), *Hyacinthoides* (bluebells), the scilla-like *Chionodoxa,* or *Ipheion,* from Argentina, with its dainty starry blue flowers.

Ground covers such as the well-known white *Alyssum* or sweet Alice (now known as *Lobularia maritima*), *Arabis, Armeria maritima* or common thrift, blue lobelia and white and blue violas and primulas would all be suitable in the foreground or as screening plants to help obscure the effect of dying foliage. Blue forget-me-nots look superb massed with tulips. Although most bulbs like dry conditions during their dormancy, ground covers help retain moisture and stop plants drying out too much during hot summers.

The addition of some yellow, a warming colour, to a blue and white colour scheme is always attractive. Any of the yellow hued *Narcissus* family would fit in with the above as would yellow violas, *Crocus* and *Lachenalia.*

Bulbs for Spring

Anemone
Babiana
Bluebell
Crocus
Grape Hyacinth
Galanthus
Hyacinth
Iris
Ixia
Lilium
Narcissus
Ornithogalum
Ranunculus
Sparaxis
Tritonia
Tulip

DAVID YOUNG

Above ◆ BLUE MUSCARI AND YELLOW NARCISSUS ARE THE LOVELIEST OF COMBINATIONS

Right ◆ CUBAN LILY (*SCILLA PERUVIANA*), WHICH ACTUALLY COMES FROM THE MEDITERANNEAN, BEARS HEADS OF INTENSE STARRY BLUE FLOWERS. BECAUSE OF ITS FLOPPY FOLIAGE IT LOOKS BEST PLANTED IN CLUMPS OR CONTAINERS. THERE IS A WHITE FORM ALSO.

DAVID YOUNG

PINK AND GREY FOR SUMMER

Low growing silver-grey plants blend well with all bulbs but in a pink and grey colour scheme they look very subtle. For a summer flowering display, lilies will make the greatest contribution. Many of them come in various shades of pink although their flower shapes will differ markedly. The sweet scented, trumpet-shaped Belladonna Lily or Naked Lady is generally available in in pink. Pink shades of alstroemeria, crinums, hemerocallis, dahlias, hippeastrums, watsonias, nerines and *Lycoris* (Spider Lily) and species and hybrid gladioli will all grow happily in the company of grey-leaved lavender, *Stachys,* feathery *Artemisia,* santolina, sage, *Dianthus, Phlomis* and *Cerastium tomentosum,* which may become invasive but is easily pulled out. Most bearded iris have greyish foliage as well.

If you wish to extend the pink and grey theme, incorporate mauve or lilac tones with the pinks. Try *Nepeta, Veronica longifolia* (commonly known as Speedwell), *Allium,* irises and *Oxali*s.

Bulbs for Summer

Agapanthus
Alstroemeria
Calla
Crinum
Dahlia
Gladiolus
Hippeastrum
Lilium
Lycoris
Nerine
Ornithogalum
Pineappple Lily (Eucomis)
Red Hot Poker (Kniphofia)
Tuberose
Watsonia
Zephyranthes

Above ♦ DAHLIAS COME IN SUCH A WIDE RANGE OF COLOURS AND SHAPES, THEY HAVE BEEN SEPARATED INTO CLASSES FOR EASE OF IDENTIFICATION. THE DAHLIA PICTURED BELONGS TO THE COLLARETTE CLASS.

Right ♦ PINK ALSTROEMERIA BLEND SUBTLY IN THIS MAINLY PINK TONED PLANTING SCHEME. AFTER WHITE, PINK IS THE MOST WIDELY AVAILABLE OF BULB COLOURS.

MICHAEL COOK

YELLOW, MAUVE AND WHITE FOR AUTUMN

The severity of your climate will dictate which bulbs you can grow in autumn. Many of the summer flowering species such as dahlia, gladiolus and hemerocallis will flower over into autumn in milder climates. They come in yellow, mauve and white.

A yellow, mauve to lilac and white colour scheme is a perfect complement to the bronze tints of autumn foliage. Try the lovely white forms of *Colchicum speciosum* and *Colchicum autumnale. Colchicum agrippinum* is a dwarf form with white or mauve checkered flowers while *Colchicum byzantinum* is mauve but taller.

Sternbergia lutea is a cheerful, yellow crocus-like bulb with dark green leaves suiting a sunny or semi-shaded rock garden or border.

Crocus flower in autumn as well as spring although some varieties need a cold climate to flower well. Those which come from Mediterranean regions however are suited to dry summers and winter rainfall. *Crocus banaticus* and *Crocus goulimyi* come in purplish colours. *Crocus hadriaticus* is a Greek species with yellow-centred white flowers.

Zephyranthes candida is a most gardenworthy plant as its leaves are attractive even when it is not in flower, making it a useful border plant. The crocus-like flowers are about 15 cm high. They are white with yellow stamens and fairly short lived. They are very easy to cultivate.

If you like pink and yellow together, nerines from South Africa are another easy-to-grow autumn flowering bulb. *Nerine bowdenii* has a pale pink delicate spidery flower which looks wonderful massed in beds or against a wall. They are good cut flowers, lasting well in water. In colder climates, as with all tender bulbs, they can be pot grown in a glass house or conservatory.

JILL KLOSTERS

Above ◆ PLANTING IRIS IN A SINGLE COLOUR IN REPEATED CLUMPS WILL ADD UNITY TO YOUR PLANTING SCHEME.

Left ◆ ALTHOUGH OFTEN REFERRED TO AS THE GUERNSEY LILY, NERINES IN FACT COME FROM SOUTH AFRICA. THE DAINTY PINK *NERINE FILIFOLIA*, PICTURED HERE, LIKES GOOD DRAINAGE AND FULL SUN. THE EVERGREEN FOLIAGE OF THIS SPECIES MAKES IT A GOOD POT PLANT PARTICULARLY AS IT MAY BE LEFT UNDISTURBED FOR YEARS. IT IS A HARDY BULB, TOLERANT OF A HOT, DRY SUMMER.

> ### *Bulbs for Autumn*
> Belladonna lily
> *Crocus*
> *Dahlia*
> *Iris*
> Spider lilies (Lycoris *and* Nerine)
> *Sternbergia*
> *Zephyranthes*

JILL KLOSTERS

RED, ORANGE, YELLOW AND WHITE FOR WINTER

Winter is the least interesting time in the garden but winter flowering bulbs in red, orange and yellow will add warmth and colour in a dull season.

Hellebores, which are also in flower at this time, combine well with bulbs that like a semi-shaded position.

In milder climates many spring flowering bulbs will make an early appearance in winter. *Galanthus* (Snowdrop) fall into this category as do the closely related *Leucojum*. Both have delicate white flowers. *Narcissus* will provide you with a creamy white and yellow in winter also.

Clivia is an invaluable shade plant in all but the coldest climates. The colourful spikes of tubular flowers come in vibrant shades of orange red and yellow. The dark green straplike foliage is very attractive and looks best planted in clumps or in borders.

Eranthis or winter aconite is a superb yellow winter flowering tuber which likes cool woodland conditions.

One of the loveliest winter flowering tubers is the cyclamen. *Cyclamen coum* and *Cyclamen hederifolium* are dependable if the conditions are right. They are low growing and small flowered but a massed display is a memorable sight. There are a number of white forms. *Cyclamen coum* has a deep crimson form.

Oxalis bulbs, which are not to be confused with the badly behaved weed, produce attractive blooms throughout the year in red, yellow, white, lavender and pink. Their clover-like foliage is an added bonus.

There are a few orange to yellow winter flowering crocus which are worth searching out.

Bulbs for Late Winter

Clivia
Convallaria
Cyclamen
Freesia
Iris
Jonquil
Lachenalia

MICHAEL COOK

Above ◆ **CLIVIA MINIATA IS A COLOURFUL SOLUTION FOR A SHADY TREE LINED PATHWAY WHERE FEW OTHER PLANTS WOULD FLOWER SO SUCCESSFULLY.**

Left ◆ **THE SMALLER CYCLAMEN SPECIES ARE DELIGHTFUL GROUND COVERS FOR A COOLER CLIMATE, WORTH GROWING FOR THEIR DAINTY FLOWERS AND ATTRACTIVE FOLIAGE.**

JILL KLOSTERS

Designing with Bulbs

BULBS IN THE COTTAGE GARDEN

Cottage gardens began as a useful collection of plants grown for cooking, perfuming the house and curing minor ailments. Vegetables, flowers, herbs were all mixed, and beds filled with annuals, perennials, bulbs and shrubs. This garden style perfectly suits today's smaller gardens, with displays of colour, foliage and heavenly scents.

Bulbs have always been included in the cottage garden where planting is traditionally haphazard, cultivation minimal and plants which reproduce themselves always welcome. The modern cottage garden, although it includes many plants unknown to the cottagers of 200 years ago, is heavily dependent on all manner of bulbs to achieve this simple unpretentious style. Daffodils and jonquils, hemerocallis, irises, freesias, dahlias, Montbretia (*Crocosmia*), squills and many others create happy profusion with traditional plants such as foxgloves and lupins, roses and lavender, delphinium and aquilegia.

Because the cottage garden evolved as a subsistence garden, herbs, vegetables and fruit trees had an important role to play. Bulbs grew indiscriminantly amongst them so that flowers, vegetables, herbs and productive trees were given equal value. This charming lack of discrimination is just as attractive in today's modern garden. However, for ease of maintenance, these cottage gardens are now planted in a more orderly fashion, though they should never look formal or regimented.

MICHAEL COOK

Above ◆ **WHITE VIOLAS, WHITE PRIMULA, YELLOW DAY LILIES (*HEMEROCALLIS*) AND MAUVE IRISES BLEND SUCCESSFULLY WITH *LAVANDULA DENTATA* IN THIS COTTAGE STYLE GARDEN.**

Below ◆ **AN ORCHARD IS THE PERFECT PLACE TO GROW SPRING FLOWERING BULBS.**

TIM SIMPSON

BULBS IN THE NATURAL GARDEN

In warm climates, competing weed growth makes it difficult to naturalise bulbous plants. In cooler climates flowering is almost over before weeds become a serious problem.

In a warm region, therefore, direct planting into turf is not advisable but attractive, simulated natural planting can be done by creating a large free-form bed with a deciduous or lightly-leafed evergreen tree. The bulbs are planted in random drifts and the whole bed heavily mulched.

The planned effect may take several years to achieve unless a large number of plants are used in the first place. Pink Windflower (*Zephyranthes grandiflora*), is one of the true bulbs which will give the most rapid results. On a larger scale, many of the iris provide a spectacular mass of colour and colonise rapidly.

To plant bulbs in turf, only a sharp rounded trowel is needed. Holes are dug out twice as large as necessary and if soil is inferior, enriched material should be substituted.

If the overall effect is to look really natural, then random planting is essential — cast a basket of small potatoes into the air, and plant the bulbs in the position where the potatoes fall.

Only bulbs such as daffodils, which can be left undivided for several years, should be used in naturalised plantings, not forgetting the initial thorough soil preparation for the holes.

Even in quite small gardens you can create a pleasant natural effect, especially in shady areas under deciduous trees. European bulbs are good 'companion' plants with deciduous trees, as they drain soil so bulbs are not waterlogged and bulbs feed in late winter, spring and summer, and receive sun and light when the trees are dormant. Bulbs also make good use of leafmould. Try planting a spring carpet of Spanish bluebells (*Hyacinthoides hispanica*) under flowering crabapples and *Prunus*; or grow Grape Hyacinth (*Muscari*), freesias, and, in a damp place, Lily-of-the-Valley (*Convallaria majalis*) for attractive effect.

Bulbs planted through other ground covers can also be beautiful. The ground cover mimimises the effect of the dead leaves and serves as useful protection, particularly for tulips which benefit from having roots shaded. For contrasts, plant up to a dozen bulbs together in small clumps for bright notes here and there, ideally against dark foliage. For this, anemones, daffodils, dahlias, gladioli, iris, lilies, ranunculi or tulips are best.

SPANISH BLUEBELLS (*HYACINTHOIDES HISPANICA*) ARE AN IDEAL BULB FOR NATURALISING IN GRASS UNDER TREES.

Designing with Bulbs

BULBS UNDER TREES AND SHRUBS

Bulbs can be such a delightful addition to the garden it is well worth taking the time to design them into your overall structure rather than including them as an afterthought. A mass planting of bulbs will complement trees and shrubs when they are flowering or highlight their trunks and foliage if they are not. Autumn flowering bulbs like crocus, colchicum, nerine, zephyranthes and sternbergia can enhance autumn tinted foliage at a time when apart from berries, little else is happening in the garden.

There are many easily grown bulbs, such as Spanish bluebells (*Hyacinthoides hispanica*) or spring starflower (*Ipheion*) which give a woodland effect, even in a small garden, if you allow them to naturalise under deciduous trees. A tree without leaves allows the winter sun to shine through at a time when spring flowering bulbs need the warmth to become active. The accumulation of fallen leaves also provides a cool and fertile haven when bulbs are dormant. If planted in grass, mowing will have to wait until the foliage has died down. Grass cut at different lengths can be very decorative however.

Cyclamen, which we tend to think of mainly as showy florist's plants, are for planting under trees. Although smaller, *Cyclamen hederifolium* (formerly *C. Neapolitanum*) and *Cyclamen coum* are invaluable plants in the winter garden. Their leaves, some silvery, are as charming as their flowers.

Lovely colour combinations can be made using bulbs under spring flowering fruit trees such as cherries, plums and crabapples. Rose pink *Zephyranthes grandiflora* which flowers in summer, will pick up the colour of the red leaves of the cherry plum. Soft pink, blue and white early spring flowering bulbs create a fairytale look planted under a blooming *Magnolia* x *soulangeana* or *M. stellata*.

Bulbs Under Trees and Shrubs

Agapanthus
Bluebells
Clivia
Crocosmia
Crocus
Cyclamen
Ipheion
Ixia
Muscari
Scilla
Tulip

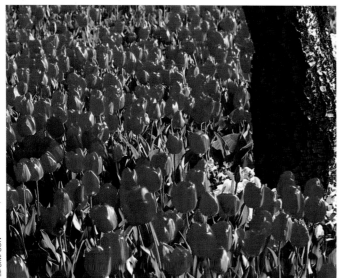

WHEN PLANTING BULBS UNDER TREES DON'T BE TEMPTED TO SCRIMP ON NUMBERS. BULBS ALWAYS LOOK BETTER PLANTED EN MASSE, AS THESE TULIPS (LEFT) AND RANUNCULUS (ABOVE).

TIM SIMPSON

MICHAEL COOK

COMBINING WATER AND BULBS IN THE GARDEN

Water is an important element in any garden. Apart from attracting birds, water always invokes a mood of tranquility or coolness in any garden setting.

Although it is true most bulbs prefer good drainage there are some, like the Water Iris, which is quite happy standing in shallow water or on the water's edge.

Louisiana Iris is native to the swamps of southern North America so it grows in damp places and tolerates humidity.

Other moisture-loving irises include *Iris sibirica* from central Europe and Russia. Its purplish blue flowers are ideal for cutting.

Iris ensata (syn. *I. kaempferi*) and *Iris laevigata* are two flat-topped varieties suitable for water-side planting. *Iris laevigata* will grow standing permanently in water whereas *Iris kaempferi* only requires moisture during the growing season. Neither likes lime.

Another well-known aquatic is the yellow *Iris pseudacorus* which Louis VII of France used for his emblem as a crusader fighting in the Holy Land, hence the name Fleur-de-Lis, a corruption of Fleur-de-Louis.

Zantedeschia (Arum Lily), *Hemerocallis* (Day Lily) and canna are all colourful and useful plants for clumping or mass planting around a pond. Cannas, so often seen gaudily mixed in public parks, are worth growing for their exotic good looks although they do require space and can be a bit untidy at times.

TIM SIMPSON

Above ♦ THE FAMOUS ENGLISH GARDEN DESIGNER GERTRUDE JEKYLL BELIEVED THE CORRECT PLANTING FOR ALL FORMAL POOLS WAS THE WATER LILY. PERHAPS SHE SHOULD HAVE ADDED IRIS AS WELL, AS TOGETHER THEY MAKE A PERFECT COMBINATION.

Below ♦ ARUM LILIES ARE EXTREMELY VERSATILE. IN THIS ITALIAN GARDEN THEY HAVE BEEN USED TO SOFTEN THE EDGE OF THIS WATER FEATURE.

JOANNE MORRIS

TIM SIMPSON

ORANGE KNIPHOFIAS AND BLUE AGAPANTHUS GIVE DRAMATIC EMPHASIS TO THIS UNSTRUCTURED DRIVEWAY.

BORDERS, BEDS, BANKS AND ROCKERIES

A ribbon planting of one bulb or a combination of bulbs can help emphasise the line of a meandering pathway or the gentle curve of a driveway or border.

Fairly tall plants like day lilies and irises are available in a wide and lovely range of colours. Agapanthus in blue or white and kniphofia in red, orange, cream or yellow are not only tough but their straplike, evergreen foliage is attractive as well.

Daffodils, bluebells and tulips always make effective borders but nerines and lycoris, which are quite similar, can be equally successful. If you live in a sufficiently warm climate, hippeastrum, often seen growing in pots (particularly in cold climates), are dramatically different when grown en masse.

Because of the good drainage offered by sloping banks and rockeries, bulbs do well in this kind of environment. Rocks provide good shelter and if a rock garden provides both sun and semi-shade then a number of different types of bulbs can be grown. Smaller bulbs, which don't demand too much water, are preferable in rockeries. Many dwarf bulbs are now available from seed. If grown from seed there can of

Bulbs for Rockeries

Alliums
Dwarf Agapanthus
Dwarf Tulips
English Bluebell
Freesia
Hoop Petticoat Daffodils
Ipheion
Lycoris
Nerine
Sparaxis
Tritonia

Bulbs for Borders

Anemone
Bluebell
Lachenalia
Hyacinth
Nerine

course be a wait of a few years for flowers. Make sure there is no competition from weeds and there is sufficient soil to plant your bulbs at the required depth. Try dwarf agapanthus, *Lycoris,* nerines, *Ipheion, Zephyranthes candida*, the smaller alliums, babiana, freesias, sparaxis and tritonia.

Use ground cover plants such as raoulias, to form a delightful carpet for small bulbs. Overplant with white or blue grape hyacinths, small alliums, narcissus or anemones. Larger plants like agapanthus, Belladonna Lilies, *Dierama*, *Dietes*, gladioli (particularly *G. callianthus*), watsonias, irises, Day Lilies, and yellow asphodel look splendid massed on banks.

Bulbs generate an informal mood planted as borders under pergolas and arbours, beside pathways and staircases, encircling statues and birdbaths. If you are fortunate enough to have a lime walk, a pear walk or a stilt hedge then an underplanting of bulbs is almost obligatory. Gardens of long ago traditionally had borders of bulbs, with the most popular ones being anemones, bluebells, Cape Cowslips *(Lachenalia),* hyacinths and nerines.

If creating a massed bed, raise the centre by several inches and ensure good drainage. Plants which are suitable for massed bed displays are cannas, dahlias, gladioli, Dutch iris and tulips. Most require annual lifting.

Right ◆ COLOURFUL POLIANTHES MAKE AN ATTRACTIVE FOREGROUND FOR TULIPS WHICH ARE RATHER STIFF IN APPEARANCE WHEN GROWN IN BEDS ON THEIR OWN.

Below ◆ THE BEDS IN THE CENTRE OF THIS CARRIAGE WAY HAVE BEEN DESIGNED WITH AN ALL WHITE THEME. WHITE STANDARD ICEBERG ROSES ARE GENEROUSLY UNDERPLANTED WITH CREAMY WHITE TULIPS 'TRIUMPHATOR' AND WHITE VIOLAS.

Bulbs for Banks

Agapanthus
Belladonna Lily
Dierama
Dietes
Gladiolus
Hemerocallis
Iris
Watsonia
Yellow asphodel

DAVID YOUNG

JOANNE MORRIS/GARDEN AT MOIDART, NEW SOUTH WALES

BULBS FOR ROOFTOPS, COURTYARDS, TERRACES AND PAVED AREAS

ROOFTOPS Bulbs are ideally suited to rooftop gardens although watering will have to be monitored as this kind of position can be windy and exposed. Planting bulbs in the protection of box hedged beds or parterres would help overcome this problem. Gardening in containers is another obvious way of dealing with these situations.

COURTYARDS Bulbs are useful plants for courtyards and terraces as these areas receive the most use and attention. It is here people sit, eat and entertain so seasonal colour and leaf pattern will be important.

The courtyard garden is an ideal place to plant small bulbs. These can be tucked into crevices or placed on the edge of the paved surface.

These areas are generally warm and sheltered with reflected heat from surrounding walls, the perfect habitat for bulbs. Evaporation is more rapid however, so heavy mulching and careful watering is necessary. Scented bulbs such as freesias, belladonna lily, jonquils, *Babiana*, iris, *Polianthes tuberosa* and the easily grown *Lilium regale* are just a few to choose from. Suitable for very warm courtyards are the small-growing Red Hot Pokers, lachenalia, *Ipheion* (Starflower) or Scarborough Lily.

PAVED AREAS Depending on the kind of paving used, smaller bulbs such as *Ipheion* and wind or rain lily (*Zephyranthes candida*) will soften and add charm if planted between paving stones or in pockets. These pockets will have to be soil enriched and mulched where possible.

Zephyranthes candida is especially valuable for a crevice as the dark, glossy, slender leaves are almost evergreen and provide a handsome contrast to the wide-open, pure white flowers with their ring of yellow stamens.

Where a pebble garden or gravelled section is used for special effect, the material can be set aside first. After the hole is dug and refilled with the soil mix and the bulb planted, the pebble or gravel can be reused as a topping over the organic mulch.

GLADIOLI ARE NOT OFTEN THOUGHT OF AS SCENTED PLANTS, HOWEVER THE NIGHT SCENTED *GLADIOLUS TRISTIS* IS EASILY GROWN IN A WARM CLIMATE.

COLOURFUL SPARAXIS NATURALISE FREELY BETWEEN PAVING STONES.

Bulbous plants suitable for this type of landscaping include babiana, freesias, Grape Hyacinths, Hoop Petticoat Daffodils, ixias, lachenalias and sparaxis.

BULBS IN CONTAINERS

There are many reasons why bulbs can satisfactorily be grown in containers such as pots, urns, troughs, tubs and windowboxes. They are the perfect answer for people who love to garden but have little space. They can be placed in positions where other plants will not grow.

In colder climates, frost is the greatest enemy of some bulbs so cultivation in pots means they can be moved under cover when necessary.

Watering and fertilising can be more easily controlled with pot culture and weeding is not a problem.

To overcome the period when bulbs are dying back and foliage is no longer attractive, many gardeners grow their bulbs in containers sunk into garden beds. This way they can be removed and taken to other parts of the garden to die back.

Containers can easily be rotated so that when bulbs are in flower they can be placed in a prominent position for their

Above ◆ *CYCLAMEN PERSICUM* IS GENERALLY GROWN AS A POT SPECIMEN. THEY ARE AN IDEAL INDOOR PLANT FOR WINTER BUT WILL NOT APPRECIATE AN OVERHEATED ROOM. THEY ARE PROBABLY BETTER TREATED AS AN ANNUAL AS IT IS NOT EASY TO POT THEM ON.

Below ◆ THE STRAIGHT-LEAVED FOLIAGE OF EVERGREEN AGAPANTHUS, TULBAGHIA, AUTUMN-FLOWERING *ZEPHYRANTHES CANDIDA* AND STARRY BLUE *IPHEION UNIFLORUM* MAKE AN ATTRACTIVE COMBINATION IN TERRACOTTA POTS.

colour and scent. If their leaves are not evergreen they can be moved out of sight while they are dying back. (Don't forget bulbs need watering and feeding while leaves remain green.) When quite dormant you can tuck them away in a cool, dry spot to await the next growing season.

Containers can be brought indoors for house decoration when flowers are at their most enjoyable stage. Bulbs planted in attractive containers also make beautiful gifts.

Bulbs like freesias, which are not too invasive and don't have to be lifted too often in milder areas, can be grown around the base of larger plants growing in tubs. Azaleas and camellias are good subjects as they are in flower at the same time as many winter and spring bulbs. If they are grown as standards, bulbs planted underneath will have a softening effect.

TYPES OF CONTAINERS Your style of house, flat or apartment will dictate what kind of container will look best for you. Generally speaking, it is better not to mix your pots in size, texture and colour too much. A highly decorative pot or container will often compete with the foliage and flowers of the bulbs you are growing. Simplicity is usually best.

Glazed or terracotta pots are always effective although terracotta dries out more quickly. Plastic pots are practical because they are lighter and easier to move. These days they come in an attractive range of shapes and colours. Good drainage is essential so make sure your containers have sufficient or adequate drainage holes and your potting mix is properly balanced and drains well. Do not allow bulbs to become waterlogged.

MICHAEL COOK

JOANNE MORRIS

Above ◆ FOR THOSE WITH LIMITED SPACE, A COUPLE OF POTS ON A WINDOW LEDGE MAY BE ALL THE GARDEN YOU HAVE. BULBS SUCH AS HIPPEASTRUMS WILL GIVE YOU BRILLIANT COLOUR FOR SOME CONSIDERABLE TIME.

Left ◆ FREESIA REFRACTA ALBA IS ONE OF THE MOST FRAGRANT OF SPRING BULBS MAKING IT AN IDEAL CHOICE FOR COURTYARD OR TERRACE.

Far left ◆ BULBS ALWAYS LOOK ATTRACTIVE IN TERRACOTTA POTS, HOWEVER TERRACOTTA DOES DRY OUT RAPIDLY AND DAILY WATERING WILL BE NECESSARY IN HOT SUMMERS. HIPPEASTRUMS ARE BOLD, TRUMPET SHAPED BULBS, PARTICULARLY WELL SUITED TO POT CULTURE BOTH INSIDE AND OUT.

When taking your pots inside don't forget to put them outside from time to time. Cyclamen do much better if they are put out for the night. Even tuberous begonias which do well indoors, like a spell outside.

Bulbs like agapanthus, clivia, hemerocallis, hippeastrums, arum and calla lilies look particularly good in large wooden tubs. Lilies are suited to large tubs as well but be careful when planting them, the less handling the better. Belladonna Lily and the lesser known Pineapple Lily (*Eucomis*) are attractive on a protected terrace.

The smaller tulips and daffodils, hyacinths, babiana, lachenalias, colchicum, crocuses and Grape Hyacinths are well suited to a sunny window box.

Nerines, lycoris, freesias, *Gladiolus callianthus*, *Polianthes tuberosa*, ixia, sparaxis and triteleia may be left undisturbed in pots for some years.

BULBS FOR PICKING

If your garden is big enough and you can sacrifice some of your bulbs for the house, there are many bulbs which last well in water. Or you may like to plant a small plot for bulbs which are to be grown for cutting only and not for garden display. There is no need to create artistic layouts and the plot will be easier to manage, to cultivate and to harvest if the bulbs are planted in rows, closer together than normally recommended, and staked where necessary to ensure straight flower stems.

The soil must be improved and a regular programme of fertilising and watering at flowering time strictly adhered to. As the flowers begin to appear, an application of liquid fertiliser at weekly intervals will improve quality, both for this season and the next.

JOANNE MORRIS

DAFFODILS, THE PROVERBIAL HERALDS OF SPRING, ARE TROUBLE FREE BULBS IN MOST SITUATIONS. WITH MINIMUM CARE THEY NATURALISE RAPIDLY MAKING THEM WONDERFUL FOR PICKING. DAFFODILS, ALONG WITH THE SMALLER FLOWERED JONQUILS, ARE PROPERLY CALLED NARCISSUS. BOTH ARE IDEAL CUT FLOWERS. PLUNGE INTO HOT WATER AS SOON AS POSSIBLE AFTER CUTTING THEN STORE IN DEEP WATER UNTIL NEEDED FOR ARRANGING.

Early morning is the best time to harvest the blooms. A sharp knife should be used so that the neck of the bulb is not injured in any way, but cut the stem as long as possible. It is preferable not to take foliage as well. The leaves are helping your bulbs to store food for next season's flowering.

Choose flowers which are in the half-open, bud stage. Place in deep water in a cool spot until time for arrangement. Flowers with bleeding stems, such as daffodils and dahlias, need to be put in hot water first. Alliums are particularly recommended for drying and are best picked with as long a stem as possible when the flowers are mature. Agapanthus heads dry well also.

Gladiolus is the most popular of the larger-flowering stems for cut flowers. It needs staking to prevent wind damage or the development of crooked stems. Other shorter-stemmed flowers such as daffodil, hyacinth or tulip will need protection from strong winds but staking is unnecessary.

Suitable bulbous plants for cut flowers include alliums, Belladonna Lilies, freesias, narcissus, hyacinths, lilies, lachenalias, hippeastrums, ifafa lilies, watsonias, gladioli, *Polianthes tuberosa*, irises, agapanthus, dahlias, clivias, Lily-of-the-Valley, anemones, crinums, galtonias, ixias, nerines, Solomon's Seal, ranunculi, scillas, calla and arum lilies.

Bulbs for Cut Flowers

Agapanthus
Alliums
Alstroemeria
Anemone
Belladonna Lily
Clivia
Crinum
Dahlia
Freesia
Galtonia
Gladiolus
Hippeastrum
Hyacinth
Ifafa Lily
Ixia
Lachenalia
Lily-of-the-valley
Lycoris
Narcissus
Nerine
Pineapple Lily (Eucomis)
Polianthes tuberosa
Polygonatum
Ranunculus
Scilla
Tulips
Vallota
Watsonia
Zantedeschia

JILL KLOSTERS

ANEMONE AND RANUNCULI ARE LOVELY FOR INDOOR DECORATION IF YOU CAN BEAR TO PICK THEM FROM THE GARDEN.

TREATMENT OF SELECTED CUT FLOWERS

Agapanthus and lilies: Plunge in water for four hours.

Dahlias: Remove leaves for 15 cm from bottom of stem.

Iris: Re-cut stems under water.

Ranunculus: Dip stem ends in boiling water then cool water for several hours.

Tuberose: Strip foliage, cut on diagonal; pinch out centre buds so plant continues to develop.

Tulips: Push wire up stem, wrap in paper and place in deep water; re-cut before using.

Gladioli: Breaks off two or three buds at top so as other flowers will open. Re-cut stems and place in warm water to open flowers.

Watsonias: Dip stem ends in boiling water then cool water for several hours.

DAFFODILS AND BLUEBELLS ARE THE MOST POPULAR OF BULBS PERHAPS BECAUSE THEY COMBINE SO WELL WITH OTHER PLANTS, AS IN THIS GARDEN.

Companion Plants for Bulbs

Because bulbs come from a wide range of habitats, from woodlands, meadows, riverbanks and rocky screes there are individual differences among them. In most cases, however, they adapt well to the company of other plants sharing the same cultural requirements. Good drainage is of prime importance to bulbs not adapted to boggy conditions. Generous mulching and water during the growing period will be fundamental to their care. More robust species like crocosmias, watsonias, *Ipheion uniflorum*, *Homeria* (Cape Tulip) and *Lilium philippinese* require less attention, however these bulbs can become invasive, a point to consider in a mixed planting.

Bulbs which do not have to be lifted frequently such as freesias, sparaxis, bluebells, narcissus, alliums, bietilla, camassia, crocosmias, dierama, erythronium, gladioli, habranthus, ixias, morphixia, nerines, tritonias or zephyranthes can be grown in front of shrubs or with ground covers and low growing plants such as violas, pansies, polianthes, primula, lobelia, alyssum, brachycome, heuchera, iberis, nemesia, and forget-me-nots. In colder climates where frosts are heavy or the ground freezes, some of these

JOANNE MORRIS, GARDEN AT MOIDART, NEW SOUTH WALES

DAVID YOUNG

TULIPS, FORGET-ME-NOTS AND RANUNCULUS IN VARIOUS SHADES OF PINK ARE A MAGICAL COMBINATION BENEATH AN ESPALIERED APPLE.

bulbs may have to be lifted and stored, in which case they need to be accessible.

Plants which don't overwhelm their neighbours are always good companions. Shirley poppies for instance are lovely with *Alstroemeria*. Bulbs, like tulips and hyacinths, which usually require lifting, are best grown either on their own or with non-invasive plants like primula, polianthes, viola or arabis.

Grey leaved plants generally blend well with bulbs. Try nepeta, *Cerastium tomentosum* (Snow-in-Summer), *Dianthus*, perennial gypsophila, *Convolvulus cneorum*, stachys (Lambs' Ears) and senscio (Dusty Miller).

Bulbs frequently have to push their way through grass in their native environment so living in close proximity with perennials like ajuga, *Phlox paniculata*, the smaller

campanulas, hellebores, arabis, armeria (thrift) and *Dianthus* otherwise known as carnation, pinks or gillyflowers, is not a problem.

Many of the cooler climate spring flowering bulbs combine naturally with spring annuals such as stock, iberis (candytuft), foxgloves, delphiniums, larkspur, wallflowers, English daisy (*Bellis perennis*), Silene (lychnis) and *Schizanthus*.

The taller flowering liliums, watsonias, irises, gladioli, galtonias, day lilies and dahlias make an elegant backdrop for summer flowering annuals such as anchusa, the summer flowering forget-me-not, canterbury bells, arctotis, cornflower, clarkia, foxgloves, helichrysum, nicotiana, nigella, oenthera (evening primrose), penstemon, rudbeckia, salvia, scabiosa, verbena and zinnia.

GROWING BULBS

Bulbous plants include bulbs, corms, tubers, tuberous roots and rhizomes. Often these are collectively referred to as bulbs. The conditions for growing bulbous plants vary but in this section is some general information on planting bulbs, including climate, soil type and preparation, mulching and watering and growing bulbs in pots. Propagating bulbous plants and solving problems are detailed here. More specific information for growing particular plants is given in the next section.

What are Bulbous Plants?

Bulbous plants are distinguished by the specialised parts below the surface of the soil that are specifically modified for food storage, and the reproduction, both vegetative and by seed, of the plant. Plants with this type of modification are almost invariably herbaceous perennials. The green, above-ground parts die down at the end of the active growing period and the plant enters a dormant stage, with buds waiting to produce new shoots at the onset of the next favourable season.

This type of modification enables plants to withstand adverse conditions during their yearly growth cycle. They are designed to survive the warm-cool cycle of temperate regions where severe winters would otherwise kill off the top growth, and the wet-dry cycle of subtropical and tropical regions where prolonged dry spells would cause dehydration and eventual death.

Bulbous plants are generally divided into five groups — bulbs, corms, tubers, tuberous roots (or swollen rootstocks) and rhizomes. These headings define whether the specialised organ of the plant is a modified stem or a modified root.

TRUE BULB

The true bulb is an underground stem that usually has a flat bun-shaped structure called the basal plate, with roots emerging around the outer edge.

The many overlapping bulb scales form the food storage receptacle, while the centre of the bulb not only contains the growing shoot, but also the embryo or unexpanded flower.

There are two kinds of true bulbs:
Tunicated bulbs: The whole structure is enclosed in a papery outer sheath that provides protection from drying out or injury. The onion and tulip are examples.

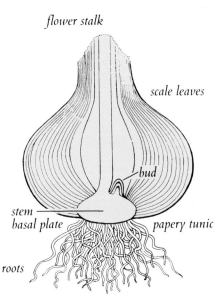

A TYPICAL BULB, AS IN NARCISSUS, HYACINTH, TULIP

Untunicated bulbs: There is no outer protective covering and the bulb has a scaly and fragile appearance, requiring constant moisture. The lily is an example.

True bulbs include *Chionodoxa, Crinum, Galtonia, Hippeastrums,* irises (bulbous type), *Lilium, Lycoris, Tulipa* and *Zephyranthes.*

CORMS

The corm is also an underground stem but whereas the bulb is comprised almost entirely of leaf scales, the corm is a short, solid, stem structure. It is usually flattened on the top and bottom and protected by the tunic covering of the dry leaf bases.

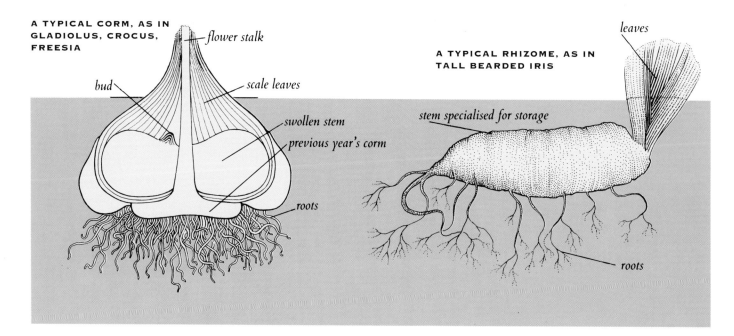

The terminal shoot bud and the flowering shoot are both at the top of the corm. As the growing season continues the plant produces leaves and flowers, using up the nutrient content of the original corm, which gradually shrivels.

The corm produces two types of roots — an anchoring, fibrous root system from the base of the old corm, and enlarged fleshy roots from the base of the new.

Plants which have corms include freesias, gladioli, ixias, sparaxis and tritonia.

TUBERS

A tuber is a swollen underground storage system with all the typical parts of a normal stem. Potatoes are the usual example, including the common potato and the sweet potato (kumara).

Tubers are formed when a variety of factors stop the above-ground growth of the plant. When this happens, roots emerge from the plant's main stem and lateral bulbs grow out horizontally. In a favourable environment the branches (called stolons) begin to enlarge and store the food manufactured by the plant above ground.

TUBEROUS ROOTS

Although the appearance of tuberous roots varies from one species to another, they all possess the features of a typical root and not a stem. Buds are at the crown or stem end and the roots are at the opposite end. Examples include agapanthus, anemone, begonia (tuberous), clivia, dahlia and ranunculus.

RHIZOMES

A rhizome is a specialised swollen stem which grows horizontally just below or on the surface of the ground and sends up leaves or stems at intervals.

There are two main types of rhizomes: some are short and thick and form a many-branched clump, tending to grow horizontally with stems arising from one side and roots growing from the lower side.

The second type has very slender rhizomes that grow continuously, spreading expansively and covering large areas.

Plants which have rhizomes include kangaroo paw, lily-of-the-valley, bamboo, banana and sugar cane.

Growing Bulbous Plants

The main time for planting bulbous plants is autumn for spring and summer flowering plants. Plant in spring and early summer for late summer-autumn flowering ones. Planting time does vary widely between different plants, so instructions from the grower on the packaging should be carefully followed.

PLANTING

A good rule for planting is to put the bulb at a depth twice to three times its size. However, South African plants like *Amaryllis* and nerines need to have the necks of the bulbs exposed, but shaded if possible. When choosing bulbs, always look for the largest, healthiest ones and plant them the right way up, usually with the point upwards. If in doubt, old roots will give the clue.

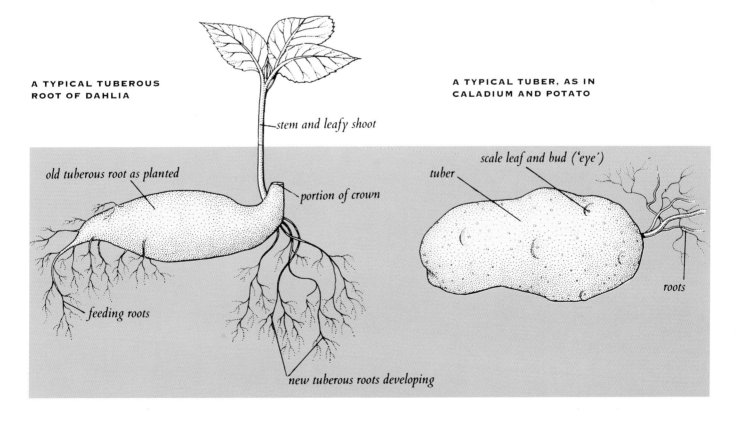

A TYPICAL TUBEROUS ROOT OF DAHLIA

A TYPICAL TUBER, AS IN CALADIUM AND POTATO

stem and leafy shoot

old tuberous root as planted

portion of crown

feeding roots

new tuberous roots developing

scale leaf and bud ('eye')

tuber

roots

CLIMATE

Although where you live generally determines what bulbous plants you can grow, many species are surprisingly adaptable to a variety of climates.

It is well to remember, however, that there will be many disappointments if cold climate bulbs like lily-of-the-valley, are attempted in a region with a warm spring and summer, or if hot climate bulbs like hippeastrum are grown in a region with a cool wet summer. Generally, bulbs need plenty of rain in the growing season and a dry period after the leaves die down.

Every bulbous plant, particularly the true bulb, requires an optimum winter or summer ripening period. Most of the spring-flowering, cool-climate bulbs require a moderately low temperature for their vegetative period — that is, the stage when the bulb grows to flowering size and attains its maximum weight. One of the main reasons for flower failure in spring bulbs after the first season is due to high soil temperature, which often prevents the flower bud forming .

Warm, wet-dry climate bulbous plants such as hippeastrums, need long dry spells to continue bulb maturity after flowering has finished. In hot conditions, at least two to three months of dryness in storage or in the ground is necessary for the growing point in the centre of the bulb to differentiate.

The right conditions can be achieved in most New Zealand and Australian gardens, even in mild to cool regions, by transferring bulbs to confined pots with well-drained soil, and sitting the pots on a hot verandah or in a sheltered area where there is maximum heat reflection from walls or concrete paths.

Most bulbous plants prefer an open sunny aspect with shelter from the worst winds.

SOIL TYPE AND PREPARATION

The ideal soil type for most bulbous plants, is a moderately fertile, sandy loam with a proportion of organic matter.

The garden bed should be dug to a depth of half a metre two or three times, with a fallow period between each digging to allow for weed seed to germinate. These weeds can then be eradicated before the next step.

Clay soil must be broken up with peat, sand and plenty of organic matter. The soil must be well worked in advance. If the soil is a heavy clay, then 15 cm of coarse sand and 15 cm of well rotted organic matter can be turned in. Sandy soil will also be improved by the heavy application of compost, manure or leaf litter.

For very poor soils, a fertiliser may be added at this stage, at the rate of 250 g per square metre. The bed should now be watered with a fine spray and allowed to settle for two or three weeks.

If drainage is inadequate, beds should be built up at least 20 cm above ground level or, if necessary, an artificial drainage system installed.

The gardener should measure each hole dug, to avoid the risk of planting too deeply or not deeply enough.

WATERING AND MULCHING

Mulching is useful in some situations, as it helps to maintain an even temperature, and helps with drainage and weeding. Quite a lot of bulbs are woodland plants that would have a natural mulch in the wild. Apart from keeping soil temperature even, it helps feed the bulbs as it rots down. It can also be used to keep temperature down, so can keep soil cool in summer. However, if bulbs need chilling temperatures in winter in borderline areas, remove mulch because it keeps soil too warm in winter.

Bulbs resent too much water so it is important to establish a balance — not too much or too little. Make sure drainage is adequate to avoid waterlogged conditions. Use mulch as this reduces weed growth (weeds can take a lot of moisture from the soil).

FERTILISING

Since most bulbs prefer a slightly acid soil, a thin layer of complete fertiliser covered by a protective layer of fine soil should be added well before planting, with no direct contact between the food and the bulb. After the bulb has been positioned, more fine soil should be pushed down gently around the bulb and well firmed. Water with a fine spray and cover with soil.

LIFTING

It is of the utmost importance to let all the leaves die down, despite their untidy appearance, before lifting bulbs. As a general rule, avoid watering once the die-down process has begun, except in the case of potted cyclamen. As the leaves die down, the plant is storing up food to promote the next season's flowers.

Not all bulbs need to be lifted after flowering. However, except in cold, hilly areas, tulips, hyacinths and gladioli should always be lifted. In cool or cold climates, tender bulbs suach as hippeastrums are lifted when leaves die down. Some bulbs multiply so fast they will need to be lifted and divided every few years. Bulbs that can be left without lifting include: freesias in mild temperate gardens (leave up to three to five years and then perhaps plant in a new spot), grape hyacinths, bluebells, rock cyclamen, both the white and pink lily-of-the-valley, Japanese iris and water lilies. Some bulbs should be left to form colonies and others that need no lifting include, autumn crocus (*Colchicum*), starflowers (*Hypoxis* and *Ipheion*) and babiana. In small gardens, space left when bulbs are lifted can be used temporarily for annuals. Some gardeners even overplant small bulbs in their dormant period but during summer, care needs to be taken not to overwater the bulbs beneath. The best way to store dormant bulbs is in a cool, dry, airy place in onion bags that let in the air and prevent disease.

POTS

Many gardeners prefer to grow bulbs in pots, especially in areas where heavy, wet garden soils prevail or where winters are cold and bulbs are tender. Careful watering and good drainage are vital. The potting mix should be equal parts loam, sand and peatmoss or leaf-mould, or bulb fibre can be used. When first planted, keep pots in cool, dark places or bury several centimetres under the soil outside. In several weeks, when the root systems are developed and shoots or buds appear, they can be moved out.

Care must be taken that snails and slugs do not attack the growing bulbs. Covering the tops of the pots with ashes, if available, will help repel these pests, otherwise snail bait must be used, or a circle of coarse sawdust placed around the pot to keep them away.

Plants that look very handsome in containers or window gardens are jonquils, tulips, hyacinths, crocuses, snowflakes, snowdrops, daffodils and *Ornithogalum*.

PLANTING BULBS

BULBS IN POTS

Check depth bulb must be planted, and size of bulb, and select appropriate pot.

For an average bulb, prepare pot first with a crock over the drainage hole (if it is a single hole pot), then add (A) a 2 cm layer of pebbles, gravel or lump charcoal if needed for better drainage; (B) a 1 cm layer of peat moss or bulb fibre; (C) a teaspoon of blood and bone or a pinch or two of mixed fertiliser; (D) a layer of sand and peat moss on which the bulb is set; (E) fill the pot with an adequate potting mixture and water regularly. Alternatively you can buy readymade bulb planting mix.

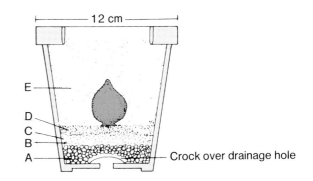
Crock over drainage hole

1 For four or five or more bulbs the pot should be 20-30 cm in diameter. Layers of planting medium are the same as before except that D will be much thicker (10-12 cm) and E will be much thinner in proportion.
2 Bulbs like crinum and hippeastrums are planted half out of the soil, one to a 30 cm pot; put potting mix with a dusting of blood and bone or mixed fertiliser, on a layer of gravel. Drainage hole covered by crock.

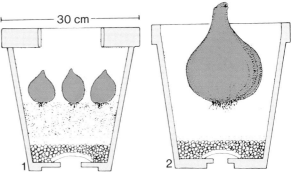

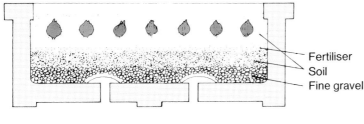
Fertiliser
Soil
Fine gravel

For shallow planted bulbs like lachenalia and grape hyacinths follow the same sequence of drainage, fertiliser and soil. Alternatively use a readymade bulb mix.

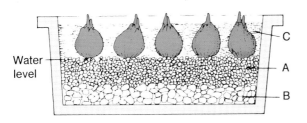
Water level
C
A
B

BOWLS WITHOUT DRAINAGE HOLE

Add (B) a 3 cm layer of charcoal; (A) a layer of gravel or bulb fibre 10-15 cm deep; (C) a layer of bulb fibre supporting the bulbs - say, hyacinths - and water level is kept to just below the bulbs. Keep the bowl in a cool dark place until roots form and shoots are well clear of the soil, then transfer to the light.

Propagation

SEPARATING BULBS AND CORMS

Dividing or separating the bulbs (called 'vegetative' propagation) produces plenty of plant material to transfer to other parts of the garden, or to pot up attractively and give away as gifts.

BULBS Hippeastrum, belladonna lily and tulip are all examples of bulbs which produce offsets. After the foliage has turned yellow, clumps are dug up, the soil gently shaken off and the offsets detached.

When bulbs are stored for the next season's planting, they should be placed in well ventilated trays in a dark, cool place, but be sure to discard damaged specimens.

CORMS The cormous plant clump is dug up, the loose soil shaken off, and the new, old and miniature corms separated. Worn out corms and dead tops are discarded.

Storage procedures are the same as for bulbs. During this period, corms which have shrivelled and become dry can be restored by soaking in warm water for a short period, then drying and dusting with a fungicide.

If very large, corms may be divided by cutting. Use a sharp knife and section the corm, making sure that each section has a growth bud. Hygienic methods are important, as cut sections are prone to rot.

DIVIDING ROOTS AND RHIZOMES

TUBEROUS ROOTS The plant to be divided may be dug up with its roots intact after the foliage has died down, and placed in a protected bed of dry material, such as sand or sawdust.

In spring, buds begin to grow near the old stem. Each root is cut off with a sharp knife, leaving at least one healthy bud and a small portion of the old stem. Discard all roots but the plump, healthy ones. Planting out is done immediately.

RHIZOMES After flowering, the whole plant is lifted with a fork and the soil shaken or washed off. Diseased parts, including leaves, must be cut off and discarded.

Individual pieces with a healthy piece of rhizome and a plump growth bud can simply be pulled apart or cut off. Choose pieces for replanting that are 7.5–15 cm, with fine, healthy roots. The amount of leaves should be reduced by half to minimise the water loss.

The detached pieces are planted immediately, almost on top of the soil, with the roots covered but half of the fleshy storage organ exposed.

SEED-SOWN PLANTS

Seeds are sown when ripe, at the stage when the seed covering is ready to split. The pods should be collected in the early morning.

Seed-sowing mixes are readily available; a reliable all-round mix can be made by using two parts rich garden loam, one part peat moss and one part clean sharp sand. If quantities are reasonably small, the mix can be baked on trays in the domestic oven at 100°C for thirty minutes to kill harmful organisms. Mix should be dampened before baking.

Seed boxes should be clean and, if necessary, scrubbed with hot, soapy water and a little household bleach added. Any type of container can be used, as long as it provides adequate drainage.

The seed-sowing medium is added to the box and firmed in, to level the surface and eliminate air pockets. Water with a fine spray.

Large seeds can be scattered thinly, but smaller seeds may need furrows to hold them. The seeds are firmed in and covered with a fine layer of dampened peat moss.

After the first true leaves emerge and the seedlings are large enough to handle without damage, transplant the seedlings into a more spacious box or into individual pots. After the new plants have flowered, cull the poorer ones.

OTHER METHODS OF PROPAGATION

LEAF CUTTINGS This method can be successful with species such as hyacinth and lachenalia.

The leaves are removed when they are well greened and mature, about the full blooming period. The whole leaf is severed at the base and can then be cut again into several pieces, depending on the leaf size.

Each leaf section is placed in the medium, with the bottom end at least 2.5 cm below the surface. Keep just damp. Within two weeks to a month, small bulbs develop on the base and roots emerge. The bulblets are then detached and replanted in rich soil.

BULB CUTTINGS This method is carried out on the mature bulbs of the daffodil, hippeastrum and lycoris.

Each bulb is cut into sections vertically, and each part must contain a piece of the basal plate.

The sections are planted in peat moss and sand, basal plate down, with only the tips showing above the surface.

Bulblets and roots develop in a few weeks, and are replanted in rich soil.

STEM CUTTINGS Experiments in propagation by using cuttings of the flowering stem have been largely confined to liliums. The cutting is made just after flowering has finished.

Bulblets form at the axils of the leaves, and produce roots and leaves while still attached to the cutting. Each piece used should have at least two nodes (stem junctions) and is inserted in a damp medium until the small bulblets form.

SOFTWOOD TIP CUTTINGS This method may be practised on plants with tuberous roots. These roots are planted in shallow soil in a warm and sheltered place and kept damp. A soft green shoot sprouts, and is cut off near the base when it reaches about 10 cm.

The lower leaves are trimmed off and the cutting is inserted in a sand and peat mix. The fragile cutting should be covered with glass, or tied up in a plastic bag with a hooped piece of wire keeping the bag away from the plant. When the tubers are well formed, the plants can be transferred to a permanent site in rich soil.

Solving Problems

OVERWATERING

The group of bulbous plants whose native habitat is South Africa (those whose storage organ is planted close to, or on top of ground level), is particularly susceptible to overwatering. These plants often do better in containers than they do in the ground — here they do not suffer quite so much from the traditional evening watering, that is the delight of many gardeners.

CLIMATIC PROBLEMS

Failure of a bulbous plant to flower in its second year can simply indicate that it is out of its climatic region.

Some attempt can be made to correct the difference in temperature, by lifting the bulbs and storing them in the crisper of a refrigerator during the period of dormancy.

When replanting, an effort should be made to keep the soil around the bulb as cool as possible by deeper planting and a much heavier application of mulch during summer (mulch should be removed in winter for bulbs which need a chilling temperature).

DISEASES

BASAL ROT One true bulb infected with basal rot (a fungal disease) may contaminate a whole clump. It appears as soft brown marks at the neck of the bulb, extending downward towards the base. Well drained soil conditions and sparse but adequate watering will help, and bulbs lifted into an airy, well-ventilated storage environment will be protected.

In rhizomatous plants, the first recognisable sign is the premature yellowing of the leaves. The disease is often associated with poor drainage, too much shade or an over-abundance of fertiliser or manure rich in nitrogen. Removal of the leaves and the affected part will arrest the spread.

VIRUSES The most common signs of viruses are yellow streaks on the leaves, streaks and splashes of colour on the flowers, and distorted growth. Some species of bulbs seem to be virus free but others including tulips, day lilies and irises are vulnerable to viruses.

Thrip infestation is indicated by white markings on blooms with dark-coloured petals, while on paler blooms a wrinkling or shrinking of the segments is detectable.

Spotted wilt affects some bulbs including *Amaryllis, Anemone, Dahlia* and *Lilium.* Symptoms vary between species. On dahlias, it shows as irregular, yellow lines on the leaves. Leaves of affected arum lilies develop yellow dots and streaks. Spraying for thrips reduces the number of diseased plants but remove weeds as well, many of which are alternative hosts. Avoid growing susceptible plants close to one another.

When buying bulbs, get a guarantee, if possible, that they are virus free.

PESTS

Failure to flower or the disappearance of the bulbous plant can also be traced to insect damage.

All lifted stock should be examined carefully before storage and then again before planting. Maggots can be destroyed without damaging the dormant bulb, by immersing it in water at a temperature of 46°C for one hour, however badly damaged bulbs should be discarded. The hot water treatment can also be used to control bulb nematodes which enter the neck of the bulb from the soil and cause the scales or leaf bases to rot.

If prolonged for three hours, this treatment will also eradicate any infestation of eelworm — transparent worms, rounded and so small as to be almost undetectable. Suspected sites of eelworm infestation should not be replanted with bulbs.

Prevention and control must be carried out at regular intervals, but even this may not be enough. If the bulbous plant is to be lifted, then storage hygiene must include preventative dusting during the period that the plant is dry and dormant.

For the control of aphids, caterpillars and other pests, preventative spraying and daily observation of blooms and leaves is a must.

Proper methods of garden hygiene generally will help you overcome a number of the minor problems of bulbous plants, and sound cultural procedures assist in preventing their occurrence.

GROWING GUIDE
Bulbs from A to Z

In general, climatic conditions in Australia and New Zealand are ideal for the majority of bulbs, although of course there are some bulbs that won't grow in extreme heat or extreme cold and so are limited to certain regions.

This guide from A to Z describes in detail and illustrates fifty of the most popular bulbs grown in Australia and New Zealand, giving a description of the plant as well as information on cultivation. For a quick guide to planting and flowering times, depth and distance apart of planting and uses, refer to the table on pages 88 to 93.

Agapanthus

(AFRICAN LILY, *LILIACEAE*)

This small genus of plants from South Africa derives its name from the Greek, 'agape', love, and 'anthos', a flower. They are widely used garden plants with fine foliage and showy flowers. Leaves are strap-shaped and arch gracefully outwards. Flowers are blue or white in many-flowered umbels, borne on long, slender leafless scapes often over a metre tall. Almost any soil suits, provided it is not waterlogged.

A. praecox subsp. *Orientalis* (syn. *A. umbellatus*) is originally from the eastern parts of South Africa. A leafy clump to 75 cm across with vigorous fleshy tuberous roots, it has many dark green, glossy, strap-shaped leaves. The blue flowers are tubular and up to one hundred make up the globular flower head on an erect leafless stem 1 m tall. Each clump may carry many flower stems during summer. This species and its varieties are more widely distributed than the true *A. africanus*, which has fewer flowers per umbel and shorter, narrower leaves. The two species are quite distinct.

A. praecox subsp. *Orientalis* var. *albus* has white flowers; plain 'Variegatus' has variegated yellow and green leaves, dwarf habit; and there is also a double blue form of *A. africanus*.

CULTIVATION These plants are easy to cultivate and thrive even if neglected. Fertilise in late winter with complete fertiliser at the rate of 40 g per square metre, with another similar dressing about October.

They will normally flower best in full sun but are decorative foliage plants in fairly dense shade. They do flower in some shade. Excellent in tubs, one large plant is sufficient for a 30–40 cm tub. The tub should be well drained, with the best soil available and specimens should be watered carefully, especially from September to December when the flowers are being formed.

In beds, new plants should be set 60 cm apart and well watered during the first six months. Remove spent flower stems and any dead leaves.

Cut flowers last well if stems are dipped in boiling water for ten to fifteen seconds immediately after cutting. Water should be changed every two or three days and a small portion of stem cut off each time.

Propagation is usually by division of clumps during late autumn to winter and early spring and is effected by digging up and pulling apart. Each new plant should separate easily, and have a sound crown and some fibrous roots. The fleshy roots may be pruned quite severely, but cut back the leaves to compensate.

The most suitable climate has moist warm conditions, which excludes some hot tropical and cooler temperate zones; also dry inland.

PLANTING SEASON: Late autumn to winter, early spring.

FLOWERING SEASON: Summer.

AGAPANTHUS ORIENTALIS

RANSOMS WILD WOOD GARLIC, ALLIUM URSINUM

Allium

(ONION, *LILIACEAE*)

A large genus of hardy bulbous herbs, mostly with a strong onion odour and spherical flowers. They are relatives of the common onion. Leaves may be broad and flat or narrow and hollow. Ornamental varieties are grown in pots, borders and rockeries. There are nearly 500 species of *Allium*.

A. aflatunense grows to almost 100 cm high with purple-lilac flowers. *A. cyaneum*, has blue bell-shaped flowers, growing to 30 cm high. *A macleanii* (previously *A. elatum*) has rosy-lilac flowers, growing to 100 cm high. *A. moly*, Golden Garlic, grows to 30 cm high with bright yellow flowers. *A. narcissiflorum* is bell-shaped with bright rose-pink flowers, growing to 30 cm high. *A. neapolitanum* produces excellent large white flowers for cutting, but should be cultivated in a greenhouse in cold areas especially where temperatures fall below -5°C. *A senescens* (syn. *A. montanum*) has starry rose to whitish flowers and grows to 30 cm high.

CULTIVATION Alliums require no special treatment. They like well drained soil, full sun, and adapt to the temperature in cool and subtropical climates. In the heat of the tropics some fail, while others could become weedy. Plant bulbs in late summer to late winter depending on the district, at a depth equal to twice their diameter. Flowers will appear in spring and summer. Propagate by seed, or by separating young bulbs in autumn or early spring.

The climate is not critical.

PLANTING SEASON: Autumn.
FLOWERING SEASON: Spring to summer.

Alstroemeria

(PERUVIAN LILY, LILY OF THE INCAS *ALSTROEMERIACEAE*)

The Peruvian lily is named after Baron Alstroemer, a Swedish botanist. The lilies have large, showy, funnel-shaped flowers in red, yellow or purple, with thick, fibrous rootstocks. These plants originate in South America with nearly all of them from Chile.

A. aurea (previously *A. aurantiaca*) grows to 100 cm and is the hardiest of the species. Its flowers are yellow to bright orange, spotted brown or red. Cultivars are available. *A. haemantha*, Herb Lily, grows to 100 cm with reddish-yellow flowers spotted purple, and green tipped. *A. ligtu*: cultivars

WILD GARLIC, *ALLIUM*

PERUVIAN LILY, *ALSTROEMERIA AUREA*

ALSTROEMERIA PELEGRINA

from this Chilean species give exciting colours of flame, cerise, orange, pink, rose and yellow; all make good cut flowers. This species is not as hardy as

A. aurantiaca. A. pelegrina grows to 30–60 cm, with individual flowers of lilac and yellow with purple spots. *A. pelegrina* var. *alba*, has white flowers.

CULTIVATION Can be grown in the garden in a warm, sunny, or semi-shaded moist but well drained spot, if protected from frost for the first winter. (In heavy frost areas, lift and store over winter or protect dormant tubers with bracken or dry peat covering.) Once established, they will thrive for years. The smooth-stemmed flowers make good cut flowers. Peruvian lilies are best bought as established pot plants because they don't tolerate root disturbance. They can be propagated by seed. This can be collected by careful breaking of the seed pods. Plant 12 cm deep in rich soil. Clumps can be divided, with care, in autumn or spring.

Moist coastal areas as far as the tropics and also milder inland areas are suitable.

PLANTING SEASON: Autumn to winter.

FLOWERING SEASON: Spring to early summer.

Amaryllis

(BELLADONNA LILY, NAKED LADY, *AMARYLLIDACEAE*)

Amaryllis was the name of a shepherdess in Greek mythology. There is only one true *amaryllis*, which is native to South Africa. Others incorrectly ascribed to the genus include *Hippeastrum* hybrids, *Sprekelia, Lycoris, Brunsvigia, Crinum, Nerine, Sternbergia, Vallota* and *Zephyranthes*.

A. belladonna, (syn. *Callicore rosea*), and others, grows to 60–75 cm in height. The lily has trumpet-shaped, rose-red, fragrant flowers in summer or autumn after the foliage has died down. The various other colour forms available ranging from white to purple are probably not *A. belladonna*, but hybrids with other species.

CULTIVATION Planting of bulbs extends from late autumn to winter, but it is better to have them planted during dormancy, usually early spring. They are hardy and thrive in a sunny position. Plant with the tops of the bulbs just above the surface of the soil, and water well during the growth period. Once established, bulbs can be divided during dormancy.

The climate is not critical.

PLANTING SEASON: Early spring.

FLOWERING SEASON: Summer or autumn.

AMARYLLIS BELLADONNA

ALSTROEMERIA

Anemone

(WINDFLOWER, RANUNCULACEAE)

Of the seventy species of this genus, only a few are commonly grown. Spring-flowering anemones were developed from tuberous species native to eastern Europe and western Asia and include *A. coronaria*, *A. hortensis* and *A. pavonina*. Many shades of colour are available in single and double forms. Two types generally available are the single-flowered series known as 'de Caen' and the doubles usually sold as 'St Brigid'.

A. x *hybrida*, Japanese Anemone, is an evergreen herbaceous perennial with three-lobed leaves and fibrous roots, but is not strictly a bulb. The many cultivars have delicate single or semi-double flowers in shades of pink, claret red, lilac, and also white on stems up to 1 m high. They are slow to become established unless planted in late winter to early spring in semi-shade. They make ideal ground cover.

A. nuttalliana, from North America, grows to 20 cm. It has solitary bluish-violet flowers, 5–8 cm across, and hairy sepals. It has medicinal value.

A. patens is similar to *A. nuttalliana*. *A. pulsatilla vulgaris*, Pasque Flower, from eastern and central Europe and Britain has an overall hairy appearance with fern-like leaves and solitary purple flowers in spring. It is still commonly used by herbalists in the treatment of nervous afflictions.

CULTIVATION Tuberous anemones are normally planted in March or April and like well drained sandy soil rich in humus, with plenty of sun. They will grow abundantly in almost complete shade. When preparing the bed, a lime dressing should be added. The tubers should be planted claws down and covered with only about 2.5 cm of soil. Seedlings should be planted out when showing two or three leaves. Water with liquid fertiliser several times during the growing season and at any sign of yellowing.

Moist climatic conditions are suitable, excluding the hot tropical areas and dry inland areas.

PLANTING SEASON: Autumn.
FLOWERING SEASON: Spring, Japanese Anemone in late summer and autumn.

BABIANA STRICTA

ANEMONE CORONARIA

Babiana

(BABOON FLOWER, IRIDACEAE)

These low-growing herbs have attractive cup-shaped flowers in lilac, blue, yellow, pink or red. The flowers grow from corms, with stiff, ribbed hairy leaves. The name is from the Dutch word for baboon because baboons eat the corms. This genus is native to South Africa.

B. disticha has pale blue flowers and grows to a height of 30 cm. *B. plicata* has lilac to violet, pale blue or white, fragrant flowers and grows to a height of 20 cm. *B. pygmaea* has sulphur yellow flowers with purple-maroon centres, on two to four spikes, which are 9 cm in height. *B. rubrocyanea* has scarlet and bright blue flowers, and is 20 cm in height. *B. stricta* grows to 30 cm tall with red, lilac or white flowers. *B. stricta* var. *sulphurea*, grows to 20 cm with pale yellow to white flowers.

CULTIVATION *Babiana* species are easily grown in any open, sunny and well drained position. They need shelter from the hot afternoon sun in dry inland areas. The freesia-like, brightly coloured flowers are particularly suited to rockeries, or cultivation as pot plants. Propagation is by seeds or corms. Corms should be planted about 6 cm deep and 3 cm apart from February to May. Flowers appear later than freesias or sparaxis, about October. Corms need to be lifted every three years.

The climate is not critical, except in cold, temperate areas as babianas are frost tender.

PLANTING SEASON: Late summer to autumn.
FLOWERING SEASON: Spring.

Begonia

(BEGONIACEAE)

This genus has over nine hundred species, and is one of the great groups of cultivated ornamental plants. Begonias are natives of tropical and subtropical climates, but it is possible to enjoy begonias in many different climates and at all times of the year, whether as bedding plants, in the greenhouse or as decorative house plants.

For horticultural purposes, begonias may be divided into three main groups: tuberous-rooted, fibrous-rooted, and rhizomatous.

Tuberous begonias are prized for their glorious double flowers. They grow in profusion in brilliant colours ranging through pink, rose, red, cerise, vermilion, salmon-orange, bronze, yellow, cream, white and a combination of these shades.

The modern, summer-flowering tuberous begonias B. x *tuberhybrida*, have been bred to attain a very large flower size and disease-resistant stems that are sturdy enough to carry the heavy flowers. Their petals show great variety, some being frilled and ruffled and resembling the flowers of hollyhocks, roses, camellias, carnations and even daffodils.

Enormous blooms up to 30 cm in diameter are found in some hybrids, but the Multiflora group has low bushy plants with many, relatively small flowers. These are more suitable for pot plants than the very large-flowered varieties. They carry their 8–10 cm flowers on strong stems clear of the foliage.

CULTIVATION Tuberous begonias may be raised from seed, leaf cuttings, tubers or tuber cuttings. Seedlings should be raised in sterile soil, with a drainage layer in the bottom of the seedbox followed by a mixture of finely sieved loam, fine sand and peat moss in equal quantities. Sow the seed thinly over the surface and press very lightly into the soil. Water by standing the box in a

IN VERY COLD CLIMATES BEGONIAS ARE OFTEN GROWN IN A HOT HOUSE

tray of cold, boiled water until the moisture creeps to the surface. Cover the seedbox with a sheet of glass or plastic and keep in a shaded place, or cover with brown paper to exclude the light.

The seedlings should start to appear within 14–17 days. Prop up the glass at one side with a small wedge when the first leaves appear, then remove the glass altogether about three days later. The seedlings should be pricked out into small pots or nursery beds as soon as possible. This is particularly important with seedlings raised in soil that has not been sterilised as begonias are very susceptible to damping-off fungus.

Dormant tubers may be started in early spring by placing them, hollow end uppermost, in trays of moist peat moss until the shoots appear. When the third leaf appears, transfer the tubers to individual 13 cm pots filled to about 2.5 cm depth with drainage material and topped with two parts each of garden loam, peat moss or leaf

mould and sand plus one part of well rotted cow manure. Keep the pots moist in a shady position protected from frost.

Alternatively, cuttings may be taken from the newly sprouted tubers. Leave the strongest shoot to become the main stem of the plant and cut out the lesser shoots as soon as they have established themselves. Make a clean cut to the tuber just below the basal ring. Crowd the cuttings into a pot filled with the rooting medium and keep them shaded and moist for about two weeks. When new growth is under way they may be transferred.

Tubers or small plants may be planted in garden beds in semi-shade in a well drained position. They prefer a rich soil with plenty of humus. Plant the tubers with the crowns no more than 12 mm below the surface. Keep them well watered but do not over-water in humid coastal areas. Do not feed tubers until they have formed roots or they will rot. Protect tubers from the hot summer sun.

Begonias should be fed only with organic plant foods. If mildew appears, spray with a fungicide, which will destroy open flowers but not buds. Sprays should only be used towards nightfall or when the temperature is below 25°C.

The best tuberous begonias for bedding are from the Multiflora group.

The trailing tuberous varieties of the Pendula group make spectacular subjects for baskets. 'Red Cascade' has a profusion of pendulous flowers; 'Betha' is salmon pink, 'Golden Shower' is golden yellow and 'Irene' is pale pink. Hanging basket varieties are sometimes listed as *Lloydii* begonias. They need warmth and humidity and plenty of organic food.

Tuberous begonias have to be lifted and stored during the winter but their normal care should continue until about May as the tubers must store plant foods for the following season. If in a frost-prone area, transfer bedding begonias to pots and keep them in a warm, sheltered position until May and allow plants to dry off. The stems may then be easily removed from the tubers. Lift the tubers from the soil and clean them, being careful to remove any remaining stem which might rot them. Dry on a rack in the sun for several days until the tubers feel firm and hard. Store during winter on racks in an airy position or in pots filled with clean, dry sand or peat moss.

The best climate for begonias is moist shady warmth or cool sun, and as far as tropics for fibrous rooted.

PLANTING SEASON: Spring.
FLOWERING SEASON: Summer.

BEGONIA X TUBERHYBRIDA FEMALE FLOWER

Canna

(CANNACEAE)

Canna is derived from the Celtic word 'cana', cane, in reference to the characteristic growth of these perennial herbs. Native to the Caribbean and South America, they are particularly suited to temperate and subtropical areas. Cannas grow 75–300 cm tall in their natural state, with very showy, terminal clusters of flowers. They are effective for mass displays and for coloured foliage and are grown in long rows in large beds such as in parks and along median strips. Some species flower for as long as nine months.

C. flaccida grows to 150 cm with 60 cm long leaves and yellow flowers. This species is the prime parent of over two hundred modern varieties available.

The dwarf cultivar 'Hungaria' grows 60–90 cm with rose flowers. 'John Lachner' grows 90–120 cm with pale bronze foliage and deep pink flowers. 'Pandora' grows 90–120 cm with red flowers. 'Richard Wallace' grows 75–90 cm with orange flowers marked yellow.

Medium cultivar 'King Humbert' grows 120–150 cm with dark bronze foliage and rich orange flowers.

CANNA INDICA

CANNA INDICA

Giant cultivar 'Florence Vaughan' grows 150–180 cm with yellow flowers spotted red. 'Centennial' grows 150–180 cm with bronze foliage and bright red flowers. 'Wentzer's Colossal' grows 150–180 cm with bronze foliage and scarlet flowers.

C. indica, Indian Shot, grows to 120 cm with 45 cm long leaves and red flowers. *C. iridiflora* grows to 300 cm with 120 cm long leaves and rose-coloured drooping flowers. *C.* x *orchiodes*, Orchid-flowered Canna, has green or bronze foliage and orchid-like yellow or red marked flowers 15 cm across. *C. warscewiczii* grows 150 cm with purplish stems, broad leaves and scarlet flowers, sometimes with blue markings.

CULTIVATION

Use richly manured soil to a depth that will accommodate the thick, branching roots. Plant at about 60 cm intervals in August or September and mulch with manure in late spring. Once blooming, give liquid manure, and always ensure they have plenty of water. To propagate, sow seed in autumn or spring, or divide the roots in winter when they should be pulled up, thinned to about four stems per plant and replanted.

The best climates range to wide moisture and temperature areas excluding inland extremes. Some protection is needed against severe frost, for example in the Victorian mountains, Tasmania and some parts of New Zealand.

PLANTING SEASON: Winter to early spring.

FLOWERING SEASON: Summer.

Clivia

(AMARYLLIDACEAE)

CLIVIA MINIATA

A brilliantly coloured South African genus that is ideal for brightening up a shady corner of the garden or under a tree. It does not require sun to thrive. Very hardy with bulbous, fleshy roots and attractive, narrow, evergreen leaves. It blooms in late winter to mid-spring usually with clusters of trumpet-like flowers carried on stiff, easily cut stems.

C. miniata, grows to 45 cm and has pale orange to orange-red or yellow flowers shaded yellow inside, in twelve to twenty flowered umbels. It makes a successful houseplant. *C. nobilis*, Cape Clivia, grows to 60 cm and has longer, more drooping spring flowers, coloured orange and tipped green, in umbels of up to sixty flowers.

CULTIVATION Plant out in autumn, just below the surface, about 30 cm apart, in a well drained position and leave undisturbed. Propagation is by division.

Massed plantings under trees on the shady side of a driveway give the best effect, but it is extremely adaptable and hardy. It does, however, require frost-free conditions. The strong root system helps to bind soils and is untroubled by competition from the roots of other plants. They perform well in large pots and the cut flowers are long lasting.

Clivias prefer a well drained soil with plenty of organic matter and a regular supply of moisture throughout dry periods. Almost any ordinary garden soil will suit them but summer shade keeps the leaves in good condition. A yearly mulch of well rotted organic matter will help to keep the roots cool and choke out weeds. An application of complete fertiliser at the rate of 250 grams per square metre in later winter and again in autumn will result in a more prolific flower crop.

Increase of plants is usually by division in spring after flowering or autumn. The clump is lifted and the soil removed by shaking or washing. The individual crowns can then be separated and set out in their permanent position about 45 cm apart with the crown well above soil level.

Many plants set seed, which is enclosed in a decorative, red-skinned fleshy berry, attractive in its own right. Seeds can be collected when the berry is soft but are slow to germinate and the resulting plants may take two or three years to flower. If neglected, clivias can become a harbour for snails and baits must be laid regularly. Damaged leaves should be cut off.

Warm to hot moist coastal to tropical climatic areas; in shade in warmer areas.

PLANTING SEASONS: Autumn.

FLOWERING SEASON: Winter to spring.

Colchicum

(AUTUMN CROCUS, LILIACEAE)

The name originates from a province in Asia Minor called Colchis, where this plant was prolific. The plant has no connection with the crocus family; the flowers, however, are crocus-like. *Colchicum* are hardy, bulbous plants to 30 cm in height. They produce leafless, coloured flowers from February through to autumn with the large, rather ungainly foliage appearing the next spring. They grow best in a cool to mild climate and are popular in rock gardens and borders in mountain regions.

C. agrippinum is the most popular species and has lilac petals with a distinct checked pattern of purplish-maroon. *C. autumnale* has purple flowers. *C. autumnale* var. *album* has pure white flowers. *C. byzantinum* has rose pink and purple flowers. *A. speciosum* has rosy lilac-purple flowers.

AUTUMN CROCUS

C. vernum (now called *Bulbicodium vernum*, Spring Meadow Saffron) is a small plant with a very dark corm and generally three strap-shaped leaves appearing after the flowers, with two or three purple blooms to each corm.

CULTIVATION Autumn crocuses require a loamy soil and like sunshine. They are ideal for awkward gaps in borders or grassy patches as they will flower as soon as the weather cools down. The bulbs are planted 7 cm deep and about 15 cm apart during summer. Water abundantly in dry weather and fertilise in early spring. Allow foliage to mature in the summer as no matter how ungainly it appears, it will die back naturally.

Moist, cool coastal and high climatic areas are ideal but plants will grow in mild temperate areas.

PLANTING SEASON: Summer.
FLOWERING SEASON: Late summer to autumn.

DIGGER'S GARDEN COMPANY

COLCHICUM BYZANTINUM

Convallaria

(LILY-OF-THE-VALLEY, LILIACEAE)

The tiny, bell-shaped flower of Lily-of-the-valley is renowned for its exquisite fragrance. It originated in Europe and Asia, and is found in North America. In natural and synthetic forms, this fragrance is an important ingredient in the perfume industry. Unfortunately, Lily-of-the-valley is difficult to grow in most areas where winters are not cold enough. The plant grows to 15 cm and has broad, blade-like leaves.

The storage organ is a creeping rhizome, growing horizontally below the ground level. Each year it sends up two leaves above a pair of scales, and a flower stalk from the axil of the uppermost leaf. The common species has two or three thick, broad, heavily-veined, green leaves. The small flowers are white, bell-like and sweetly perfumed and grow in racemes on a leafless stem.

C. majalis is the most widely grown species and has white flowers. *C. majalis*

'Fortunei', has larger flowers and foliage. *C. majalis* var. *rosea* is a pink flowered form.

CULTIVATION Lily-of-the-valley thrives in woodland conditions: rich soil, semi-shade and adequate moisture. The bulbs or 'pips' are planted out in early winter and every year thereafter should be top-dressed with peat or leaf mould. Do not attempt to grow this plant outdoors in tropical or warm temperate climates as disappointment is inevitable. Indoors it can be grown from pips (rhizomes) specially forced by growers. The pips are planted, with just the tips showing, in peat moss. They are then kept in a dark, moist place for a week and watered regularly. Gradually they are exposed to more light and about two weeks after planting are placed into normal light, but not heat or direct sun. They will start flowering about a week later. Propagate by seed or by dividing existing clumps in spring or autumn.

This genus is suitable only for climates with a cool spring, and a cold hard winter to get the plant blooming.

PLANTING SEASON: Autumn.
FLOWERING SEASON: Late spring.

CONVALLARIA MAJALIS

Crinum

(CRINUM LILY, VELDT LILY,
AMARYLLIDACEAE)

These lily-like, herbaceous plants with white, pink or red flowers are grown from a large bulb. Native to tropical countries, they are called lilies, although strictly they do not belong to the lily family. The Greek name 'krinum' means a lily. *Crinums* resemble *Amaryllis* and *Hippeastrum* but have long, slender flower tubes longer than the flower segments, and a clump-forming habit.

C. amabile grows to 100 cm with strap-like leaves and red, strongly perfumed flowers. *C. americanum*, Southern Swamp Crinum, from North America, has very fragrant flowers, and grows to 60 cm with showy white flowers. *C. asiaticum*, Poison Bulb, has broad leaves, a clump-forming habit and numerous greenish-white, drooping, fragrant flowers. *C. augustum* grows to 1 m with strap-like leaves, deep wine-red flowers of a paler colour inside and a light fragrance.

C. bulbispermum (syn. *C. capensis* or *C. longifolium*) has narrow leaves and funnel-shaped, white or pink flowers. It is one of the most common garden crinums. *C. campanulatum* grows to 120 cm with linear leaves, funnel-shaped, light red flowers. *C erubescens* has thin leaves and flowers in the form of long, curving tubes, white inside, purplish outside.

C. fimbriatulum grows to 100 cm with narrow leaves and funnel-shaped flowers, coloured greenish-white with red stripes. *C. flaccidum*, Darling Lily, is a herbaceous Australian species with white, trumpet-like flowers, 30 cm. *C. jagus* grows to 100 cm with broad leaves and large flowers with tubes to 15 cm. *C. kirki* grows to 120 cm with strappy leaves and funnel-shaped flowers, a greenish colour with red keels. *C. kunthianum* grows to 100 cm with flowers composed of a long white or purple tube.

C. latifolium var. *zeylanicum*, Milk and Wine Lily, grows to 60 cm with broad leaves and many funnel-shaped, white, fragrant flowers with broad red keels. *C. moorei* is a larger plant than *C. bulbispermum*, with rose-red flowers. *C. moorei* var. *album* has white flowers.

C. pedunculatum is an Australian native crinum. It grows to 100 – 150 cm with thick, strappy leaves and flowers that have a green tube and white segments. *C. podophyllum* is a small species growing to 30 cm with white flowers. *C. x powellii* is a hybrid that grows to 120 cm in height, with pink to rose flowers. *C. sanderianum* grows to 60 cm with thin leaves and white flowers with red keels. *C. scabrum* is a herb that grows to 60 cm. It has narrow leaves, funnel-shaped white flowers with red keels, and greenish tubes.

CULTIVATION Once established in the garden, Crinum will form large clumps. For the growing period they like rich soil and moisture, but have a semi-dormant winter period when watering is unnecessary. Propagate by offsets from bulbs, rarely by seed, which takes two to three years to flower, or by division of clumps.

Temperate areas, subtropical to tropical coast climatic areas, with high summer rainfall. Elsewhere grow under glass.

PLANTING SEASON: Autumn to spring.

FLOWERING SEASON: Summer.

DIGGER'S GARDEN COMPANY

CRINUM

Crocosmia

(MONTBRETIA IRIDACEAE)

Named from the Greek 'krokos', saffron, in reference to the smell of the dried leaves when steeped in water; there are five species and one well known hybrid in the genus. *Crocosmia* is very closely related to *Tritonia,* and is sometimes included in it. These hardy plants are native to South Africa, and produce summer flowers excellent for cutting.

C. aurea, Coppertip, has iris-like leaves, grows from corms to 100 cm tall and produces yellow flowers turning reddish. *C. x crocosmiiflora* (*C. aurea* x *C. pottsii*), Montbretia, grows to 100 cm and has large, bright orange-red to yellow flowers.

Cultivar 'Emily McKenzie' has large, orange-red flowers with brown markings. 'James Coey' has deep orange-red flowers. 'Lady Oxford' is one of the tallest, with pale yellow flowers. 'Rheingold' has pure yellow flowers.

C. masonorum grows to 100 cm and has orange-red flowers. *C. pottsii* grows to 100 cm and has orange-yellow flowers.

CULTIVATION *Crocosmia* species grow best in sandy loam, but they are hardy plants and like sunny positions with good drainage. Corms should be planted in early spring, 8 cm apart and 6 cm deep. They can be left to form clumps but it is best to divide about every three years. They can also be propagated from seed.

Most climatic conditions are suitable, excluding hot tropical and dry inland areas.

PLANTING SEASON: Autumn, winter or spring.

FLOWERING SEASON: Late summer.

CROCOSMIA

Crocus

(IRIDACEAE)

There are about 80 species of the genus *Crocus*, a cormous plant that is native to the Mediterranean region, southern Hungary, the Balkans and Asia Minor. Although most types flower in late winter or early spring, species like the lavender-coloured *C. speciosus* and the violet-purple *C. sativus* flower in autumn.

These winter and autumn blooming cormous herbs with grass-like leaves and flowers of white, yellow or lilac derive their generic name from the Greek work 'krokos', saffron. The familiar and easily grown garden hybrids are mostly of Dutch origin. Crocuses flowering in autumn are sometimes confused with *Colchicum*, which are known as autumn crocuses, but *Colchicum* belongs to the lily family. The commercial saffron used for colour and flavouring comes from the dried red-yellow-orange stigmas of the Saffron Crocus, *Crocus sativus*.

C. sativus, Saffron Crocus, is the source of a yellow dye used since antiquity in the Mediterranean lands and in the Middle East to colour royal robes. It is still cultivated on a large scale for this purpose in southern France, Spain and Turkey. The dye is prepared from the conspicuous feathery orange stigmas.

Crocuses have small flat corms and the cool-climate types, including most of the Dutch hybrids, seem to require a prolonged cool growing season after the flowers have finished to encourage the corms to multiply.

The leaves of crocuses are green, fine and slender. The flowers are shaped like a chalice, or sometimes a globe, on short stems up to 10 cm long. The flowers, which open up in a flattish circle of petals, are in shades of blue, yellow, white and purple, many with conspicuous feathery stigmas.

CROCUS TOMASINIANUS

CROCUS TOMASINIANUS

Autumn Flowering: *C. ochroleucus*, growing to 8 cm has pale cream flowers with orange throats; flowers in late autumn. *C. salzmannii*, growing to 6 cm, has silvery-lilac flowers. *C. sativus*, Saffron, grows to 12 cm and has lilac flowers with a purple base and long, bright stigmas; dried, powdered stigmas produce saffron. *C. speciosus*, growing to 12 cm, has flowers of bright lilac, feathered purple. Cultivar 'Albus', white flowers with scarlet stigmas; 'Artabir', light blue flowers with striped veins; 'Cassiope', blue flowers with yellow bases to petals; 'Conqueror', sky blue flowers; 'Globosus', bright blue flowers late in autumn; 'Oxonian', deep violet blue flowers. *C. kotschyanus* (syn. *C. zonatus*) grows to 8 cm with rosy-purple flowers.

Winter Flowering: *C. augustifolius*, cloth of gold, grows to 8 cm and has deep orange flowers, brown on the outside. *C. biflorus*, Scotch Crocus, grows to 10 cm with white to lilac flowers. Var. *argenteus*, lilac with purple featherings; *parkinsoni*, creamy with purple stripes; *albus*, pure white outside flowers. Cultivar 'Silver Fairy', silvery-white flushed lilac; 'White Lady', pure white. *C. chryanthus*, growing to 5 cm with bright orange flowers feathered bronze. Cultivars are numerous, including 'E. A. Bowles', buttercup yellow; 'Snow Bunting', white; 'Zwanenburg Bronze', deep yellow, bronze inside. *C. flavus*, growing to 10 cm, has golden yellow to orange flowers. *C. imperati*, growing to 8 cm, has purple flowers with fawn on the outside and purple feathers. *C. tomasinianus*, growing 6–8 cm, has lavender to purple flowers shading to pale grey on the outside. Cultivars include: 'Barr's purple'; 'Lilac Beauty'; 'Ruby Giant'; and 'Taplow Ruby'.

Spring Flowering: *C. flavus* (syn *C. aureus*) has orange-yellow flowers. It seeds freely and is suitable for warmer climates. *C. ochroleucus* has white flowers with orange at base of petals. Its corms increase rapidly. Best grown in warmer climates. *C. vernus*, Dutch Crocus, grows to 8 cm with white to purple, sometimes feathered flowers; a variable species. *C. versicolor* var. *picturatus*; growing to 10 cm, has white flowers with purple featherings. Cultivars of the large Dutch Crocuses, growing to 12 cm and flowering in early spring, include 'Jeanne d'Arc', white flowers; 'Kathleen Parlow', pure white flowers; 'Little Dorrit', silvery lilac flowers; 'Pickwick', silvery blue flowers with deep lilac stripes; 'Queen of the Blues', lavender flowers with purple at base; 'Remembrance', soft purplish-blue flowers.

CULTIVATION Crocuses are ideal for naturalising in a semi-shaded cool spot. They can be planted in troughs and pots, and look charming in cool rock pockets or at the foot of shaded banks.

Crocuses are not particular as to soil but crumbly sandy loam suits them best, as long as plenty of well rotted organic matter is added before planting. Liquid fertiliser applied just before flowering time will help to increase the number of blooms.

Most crocus are multiplied by separation of the corms as some do not set viable seed.

They are usually fairly free from pests and diseases, providing they have adequate drainage.

Crocuses will grow in most soils and in partial shade, but do best in full sun, in light, rich soil with good drainage. They will grow well amongst grass in rockeries, or in pots. Plant the corms about 6 cm deep and apart in spring for autumn or winter species, but plant in autumn for spring species. Leave undisturbed unless they become overcrowded. Corms can be lifted when the foliage has died down. Seed can be sown in autumn, and left undisturbed for two years, when corms planted out will flower. Crocuses grow well in pots, but do not like artificial heating.

Moist, cool coastal and high climatic areas are suitable.

PLANTING SEASON: Autumn.
FLOWERING SEASON: Autumn to spring.

CYCLAMEN PERSICUM 'ROCOCO'

Cyclamen

(PRIMULACEAE)

Cyclamens are amongst the most charming of the winter flowering indoor plants. Their colours range from cyclamen through to plum reds, purple shades, pinks, salmon and many fancy whites. Variations in petal margins and leaf markings are infinite. They are well matched by the loveliness of the reflexed flowers which stand clear of the leaves on purple-tinged petioles.

In history, cyclamens were known as sowbread. When dried and ground they formed a herbal for the treatment of jaundice and similar ailments which was reputedly successful in treatment of the lovelorn. *Cyclamen* species grow naturally from north Africa throughout the Mediterranean into Italy and southern France and comprise a likely seventeen species.

C. persicum has become more familiar than others. Seeds suppliers and nurseries offer a number of named Cyclamen strains including 'Pink Pearl', deep salmon; 'Bonfire', scarlet; 'Salmon King', pale salmon-pink; 'Afterglow', cherry pink; 'Rose Queen', deep salmon and 'Mauve Queen', purple-mauve.

CULTIVATION The species *C. coum,*, *C. hederifolium* and *C. purpurascens* can be grown in woodland conditions similar to their native environment. These are cool to cold nights, warm to hot days and regular but not massive downfalls. In such climates Cyclamens can be sown as wildlings and allowed to remain in the soil after each flowering. They will reappear in time to bloom all through winter and spring.

Given the right treatment, *C. persicum* should flower right through to spring, only ceasing to form buds when the weather grows too warm. When that happens the foliage remains on the plant a further six to eight weeks before dying down. The plant should then be put to rest in a shady spot in the garden. Occasional watering should continue until autumn when it can be repotted.

All growth comes from a corm, which does not increase by offset but does increase in size each year. If watered regularly but sparingly around the edges of the pot and not directly onto the corm, rotting is unlikely. Cyclamens dislike indoor heating and draughts. They like a sunny, airy but cool atmosphere indoors.

Plants which have been allowed to go to seed are considered not worth retaining. They are easy to raise from seed but as it takes 12 to 15 months for a plant to bloom from seed, most are bought as corms ready to plant or as plants in bud. When potting corms, use a pot mixture of peat moss, sand and leaf mould and take care to plant the corm so that the top is above the soil. Cyclamen mite attack can be successfully dealt with by spraying.

PLANTING SEASON: Late summer to autumn.

FLOWERING SEASON: Late winter to early spring.

CYCLAMEN PERSICUM

Dahlia

(DAHLIA, _COMPOSITAE_)

DAHLIA

A Swedish botanist, Andreas Dahl, has been credited with the discovery of the dahlia. However, records show that the genus was actually discovered in the mountains of Mexico by a Spanish physician of the 17th century. About 150 years later Dahl, obtained some seed of this plant and became so interested in its culture and development that the name _Dahlia_ was given to this plant in his honour.

Today we have decorative, garden or hybrid cactus, exhibition cactus, show, pompone, colarette, charm and the ever-popular nymphea or water lily type dahlias. Every division has variations or types. The decorative dahlias include miniature, medium, large and giant. Miniatures are 10–15 cm in flower diameter, medium are 15–20 cm in flower diameter, large flowers are 20–25 cm in diameter and giant are over 25 cm. Cactus dahlias are divided into three flower size groups: miniature, 12–15 cm; medium, 15–18 cm; large,

over 18 cm. Hybrids should be broad at the base of the petal at the back of the flower and quilled for two thirds of the petal. Flowers of exhibition cactus should be over 15 cm in diameter, and must have long, narrow, revolute petals, quilled from base to apex. Collarette dahlias are very attractive and have one or more series of flat ray florets of eight 'petals' each; above each series is a ring of florets (the collarette) half the length of the rays and usually of a different colour. They must be over 8 cm and under 12 cm. The petals forming the collar should be uniform. Pompone blooms should be round like a gold ball and are shown at 3.75–4 cm; show dahlias are like a large pompone and should be 7–11 cm; and charm dahlias are 7–15 cm in diameter. The size of a nymphea or water lily type dahlia should be 11–15 cm, and have at least three rows of petals, but not more than six rows fully opened. The centre of the bloom should be dome-shaped and the petals must be broad and well shaped.

The dahlia blooms in summer and autumn but produces much better quality flowers, richer in colour, when the flowering period is planned for February, March and April. The tubers may be planted from spring to the end of January. The average time from planting to flowering is 14 to 15 weeks.

DAHLIA TYPES

Decoratives: Large flowered cultivars include 'Arthur Haubley', lavender rose; 'Bill Ormon', yellow; 'Honor McLaughlin', red; 'Morocco', apricot; 'Mrs A. Woods', lavender pink; 'Reta Easterbrook', blood red;. Medium flowered include 'Dorrie Evans', cherry red; 'Eagle Rock', bronze to gold; 'Hazel Morgan', orange; 'Joy Burkett', white; 'Mavis Ann', cyclamen and white. Cultivars producing small flowers include 'Freckles', yellow and red; 'Muir's Choice', salmon pink; 'Terry', rose pink; 'Andrea Dogron', wine; 'Sunset Glow', sunset shades.

Hybrid Cactus: Large flowered cultivars include 'Town Topic', purple and white; 'Broadway Melody', yellow;

DAHLIA 'GEERLING ELITE'

'Bert Goodwin', yellow; 'Dural Gold', gold; 'Molly's Pink', pink; 'Marcia Reeves', red; 'Juanita', plum. Amongst the medium flowered cultivars are 'Lady Bonython', rose pink and yellow; 'Lawson', brown; 'Memories', mauve pink; 'Vita', puce; 'Rene', maize; 'Uralla Surprise', white; 'Youth', pink. Small flowers include 'Desert Lodge', salmon pink; 'Dorothy', white and pink; 'Mrs V. Stroud', lavender; 'Oriental', scarlet and yellow; 'Rose Fletcher', pink; 'Valetta', white. *Nymphea*: Cultivars include 'Amy', yellow overlaid orange; 'Audrey Baker', pink flowers; 'Glamour Boy', red flowers; 'Orange Leader', orange flowers; 'Red Velvet', red flowers; 'Shirley Erin', pale apricot flowers; 'Valentine', gold flowers.

Collarettes: Cultivars include 'Summit', white flowers overlaid with magenta; 'Bulimba', brown and gold flowers; 'Adele Callet', dark red and white flowers.
Pompones: 'Little Willo', white flowers; 'Little Marvel', red flowers; 'Margaret John', orange flowers; 'Ralf', yellow flowers, 'Janice Mulholland', pink flowers.

CULTIVATION *Soil*: Dahlias are not gross feeding plants; too much manure will produce sappy, succulent growth and too much nitrogenous fertiliser, such as poultry manure or sulphate of ammonia, will produce vigorous top growth at the expense of the flowers. The dahlia comes from a hot, high, dry climate and therefore needs well drained soil and a sunny position. However, dahlias require ample moisture during the

whole of the growing period, but over watering must be avoided. Sandy soil that does not hold any moisture should be built up with well rotted compost or leaf mould. Some sand added to heavy soil is a good idea also. Lime or dolomite should be applied generously at least a month before any animal manure is added, working well into the soil. Dahlias are commonly grown in masses rather than singly, but there is no reason why they should not be grown as specimens in the garden.

Staking: The stakes should be set in position before planting the tubers. These are placed about 100 cm apart and the dahlia is planted in the middle, so that two stakes can support one dahlia.

Planting: Tubers are planted earlier than the green plants. If growing from tubers, a fork is the best tool to use when digging up the dahlia clumps, being very careful not to break or damage the tubers. Wash all the soil away from the tubers with a good spray of water and allow the tubers to dry off, then store them for the winter. The best method of storing is to place them in a well drained bed, up against a fence or under a tree, cover with sand and give them a good watering, and after that a light watering every two to three weeks. Any unwanted growth which is produced may be cut off 2–3 cm from the tubers a few days before dividing the clumps.

To divide the clumps, use a sharp knife and a pair of secateurs, making sure the cut is made between the tubers; each tuber should have an eye and a piece of the old stem. It does not matter how small the tuber planted, providing it is from healthy stock and has an eye.

Pinching: For the best results, one should pinch or cut out the centre of the plant, after it has grown to about 40 cm high, has developed three or four pairs of leaves, and the side growth, or laterals, are starting to grow. Pinching also helps to stop the bushes from becoming too tall. The six laterals will grow and form six leaders, resulting in a thick shrubby bush. In turn, it will stand up well, carry the heavy load of foliage and flower late in the season. Unless the season is excessively hot and dry, do not over-water tubers. Two or three good waterings a week is enough until the buds appear, then they require more water. Early morning or late afternoon is the best time.

Tying: As dahlias are brittle, tying them for support is a must. After the first tie when plants are about 30 cm high, the bushes seem to grow very quickly. It is always necessary to have at least three ties around the bushes to keep them upright. Use raffia or twine, tie to the stake, not the plant, loop around the bush and tie onto the other stake.

Disbudding: This is essential if large, quality blooms are desired. The top or terminal bud is the first to develop a little ahead of either side bud. Leave the bud which has the largest stem and cut off the other two.

Pests: The worst enemy is red spider, followed by sucking insects such as canary flies, thrips and aphids, cut worms, slugs and snails. There are low toxic sprays available

DAHLIA 'GOUTTE DE SANG'

to control these. Any fungal diseases can be controlled by sulphur or any fungicide. Stunt, mosaic, spotted wilt and virus diseases are incurable. The main symptoms are dwarfing, mottling and curling of the leaves and all infected plants should be dug out and burnt. To avoid such problems and to control pests easily, spray plants every two to three weeks from the start of growth.

Weed control: A light hoeing on a hot day will kill most of the small weeds, but remember that dahlias are surface rooted so do not hoe very deeply. A good mulch will help to keep the weeds down and also keep in some of the moisture.

The best time for picking dahlia flowers is early morning or late in the evening. Pick the flower with a good length of stem or stalk, and remember the more flowers are picked the better later flowers become. After picking the flowers, dip the bottoms of the stems into boiling water and then in cold. This ten to twelve second process seals the bottom of the stems.

The dying down period of the dahlia starts around May and it is advisable to let the bushes die down completely before attempting to lift them. At the end of June or early July, cut off the dead or dried branches leaving them 15 cm above the ground, and making sure that the first ties around the plant are removed.

The climate is not critical.
PLANTING SEASON: Spring.
FLOWERING SEASON: Summer, autumn.

Dierama

(ANGEL'S FISHING ROD, FAIRY FISHING ROD, WAND FLOWER, *IRIDACEAE*)

These hardy South African plants with roots like corms, have long, sword-like leaves and graceful, arched flower stems.

D. gracile grows to 50 cm and has strap-like leaves and mauve, funnel-shaped flowers on nodding stems. Its flowers have a dark purple spot at the base. *D. pendulum*, Fairy Fishing Rod, grows to 100 cm or more with long, pendulous flower stems and 3 cm, pink to lilac, autumn flowers. *D. pulcherrimum* grows to 100–200 cm and has nodding, rose-red flowers. *D. pulcherrimum* var. *album* has white flowers. Many other named varieties include a group of hybrids raised in Northern Ireland. 'Heron' is wine-red, 'Skylark' is violet and 'Kingfisher' is mauve-pink.

CULTIVATION Propagate from seed, by offsets produced in spring, or by dividing clumps of corms in autumn and replanting. Plants resent division but will recover in six months or more. Plant out in spring. Preference is for rich, well drained soil. Although hardy to the cold, they require some wind protection.

Moist, cool to warm climatic conditions will be tolerated, excluding hot tropical and cold, high extremes.
PLANTING SEASON: Late autumn.
FLOWERING SEASON: Late spring.

DIERAMA

Eucomis

(PINEAPPLE LILY, *LILIACEAE*)

A tuft of leaves crowns the flower spikes in the ten species of this half-hardy bulbous genus from South Africa. A single flower spike rises from a rosette of thick leaves and is densely covered with small, six-petalled flowers ranging from cream and green shades to pinkish-purple. The spike is topped with a pineapple-like cluster of leaves (strictly leafy bracts), hence its common name. *Eucomis* species are attractive feature plants for the garden and the flowers are long-lasting even when cut.

E. autumnalis (syn. *E. undulata*) has long, strap-shaped, wavy-edged leaves and spikes 50–60 cm. It carries pendant, bell-shaped, greenish flowers in late summer and autumn. *E. bicolor* grows to 75 cm and has green flowers with purple margins from February to March, surmounted by a large tuft of leaves. *E. comosa* (syn. *E. punctata*), Pineapple Flower, is an attractive plant with long, lanceolate, wavy-edged leaves, spotted with purple beneath,
and fragrant cream and green flowers. Varieties have pinkish-purple flowers.

E. pole-evansii, an outstanding species, has spikes growing to 200 cm, the top 60 cm being encircled with wide open, soft green flowers with cream centres. *E. regia*, King's Flower, has long, tongue-shaped, green and purple leaves and green flowers on a purple spotted stem in early spring.

CULTIVATION These lilies are easy to grow. In very cold districts the dormant bulbs may be lifted and replanted in spring. Bulbs set out in the garden should be planted level with or immediately below the soil surface in a well drained, warm and sheltered position in full sun. They make effective pot or tub specimens and during September, may be potted up in a compost of sandy loam with half its quantity of well decayed manure and sand. Give plenty of water during summer but water very lightly during winter. Occasional feeding with weak, liquid manure or soluble, organic plant food may be given once the flower spikes appear. The plant may be increased by removing the side shoots or offsets which develop around the parent bulb.

The climate is not critical.

PLANTING SEASON: Autumn, winter to early spring.

FLOWERING SEASON: Summer.

PINEAPPLE LILY, *EUCOMIS*

Freesia

(*IRIDACEAE*)

Named after Dr F. H. T. Freese of Kiel, this genus of a few species of South African, cormous plants are extremely fragrant. Many hybrids offer colours ranging from creamy white through yellow, orange, red, purple, apricot, brown, lavender and blue. They are low growing plants with short, strap-like leaves, with the erect flower spikes appearing in late spring several centimetres above the leaves. The flowers are funnel-shaped, about five to seven on each stem, and 5 cm long.

E. refracta, so-called because of the angled stem, is a low, tufted plant which grows to about 45 cm and bears greenish-yellow flowers in late winter and spring. A great many cultivars are available in a wide range of colours.

CULTIVATION This extremely hardy plant requires little attention apart from protection from severe cold. (In cold

Above ◆ **FREESIA REFRACTA**

Right ◆ **FREESIAS**

Top right ◆ **FRITILLARIA MELEAGRIS**

climates, corms can be lifted after flowering and ripening.) However, a good mulch of manure or compost and regular water will produce more abundant flowers. Freesias like an open position in full sun, but they will tolerate partial shade, and are excellent in forgotten parts of the garden. Corms can be left in the ground for years, but for better flowers they should be lifted and rejuvenated every three to four years. Freesias make good cut flowers. They are propagated by seed sown in a good seed mixture in January or February, scattered in rows and raised in a cool, shaded position. Plant out when big enough to handle. More frequently, corms are planted during February and March, having been collected from an old clump after the foliage has died down in late summer.

Cool to warm southern temperate and mild inland climatic areas.

PLANTING SEASON: Autumn.
FLOWERING SEASON: Spring.

Fritillaria
(LILIACEAE)

There are about 100 species of this genus. They are native to North America, Europe, Asia and North Africa.

Fritillaria imperialis, Crown Imperial, is a native of Iran and is the most striking species. It has a large bulb and the stem grows to over 100 cm. The terminal umbel, which grows from the stem, bears numerous roughly bell-shaped flowers. The flowers are pendulous and 5 cm long. They are coloured a deep yellow to bronze-yellow or more commonly orange-red.

There are many cultivars of *F. imperialis*. 'Aurea' has red-orange flowers. 'Lutea' has clear yellow flowers. 'Maxima' is a strong plant with orange-red flowers. 'Rubra' has large red flowers.

DIGGER'S GARDEN COMPANY

F. meleagris, Snake's Head Fritillary, is a native to the United Kingdom. This perennial grows to a height of 15–30 cm. The stem is erect and the leaves are long and narrow. The hanging bell flowers are rosy mauve, chequered with a dusky purple — like a snake's skin.

CULTIVATION These species will grow well in pots. Plant the bulb in an 18 cm pot with standard potting mixture. Cover it firmly with 10 cm of soil. It will not begin to grow until early spring. As soon as growth begins, start watering the plant regularly.

Most fritillaries are hardy and comparatively easy to grow in good garden soil given the right conditions, that is, cool winter as in Tasmania and the South Island of New Zealand, sun in the winter-spring growth period and a drier but not too sun-baked period when bulbs are dormant. Lift and divide bulbs every few years. Propagation is usually by offsets and not by seed.

Cool temperate and cold climatic areas are suitable for these species.

PLANTING SEASON: Autumn.

FLOWERING SEASON: Spring.

DIGGER'S GARDEN COMPANY

FRITILLARIA IMPERIALIS

SNOWDROPS, *GALANTHUS NIVALIS*

Galanthus

(SNOWDROP, *AMARYLLIDACEAE*)

Galanthus should not be confused with the taller growing *Leucojum*. The small, white, single or double flowers hang from the stalks rather like little hats, with well separated petals, and the narrow, basal leaves are 12–25 cm long.

G. caucasicus grows to 15 cm and has plain, white, rounded flowers in early spring. *G. elwesii* grows to 15–30 cm and is another early bloomer. *G. nivalis*, Common Snowdrop, has single flowers with green-tipped petals, borne on 15 cm stems. *G. nivalis* 'Flore-pleno', has double flowers. *G. plicatus*, Crimean Snowdrop, grows to 20 cm with largish flowers with green markings.

G. byzantinus (now classified as a subspecies of *G. plicatus*) grows to 22–30 cm, has broad, dark green, 12 cm leaves and is among the largest flowers of the species, with green marks at the base of the inner segments.

CULTIVATION *Galanthus* species, which should be planted in a cool, partly shady spot, are easy to grow in a light soil. Plant the bulbs in February, 5 cm deep and 5 cm apart.

Moist, cool coastal and high climatic areas are suitable for this genus.

PLANTING SEASON: Autumn.

FLOWERING SEASON: Winter, spring.

Galtonia

(SUMMER HYACINTH, *LILIACEAE*)

Very like the hyacinth but much taller, this perennial South African bulb plant is suitable for the back of a border. The bell-like flowers are greenish-white and bloom in summer in single, spiky racemes.

G. candicans, Summer Hyacinth, grows 60–125 cm, with leaves up to 100 cm long and 5 cm wide. The summer blooming flowers are pure white, 2–4 cm long and have a sweet smell. *G. princeps* is similar to *G. candicans* but with shorter scapes. Its flowers have a greenish tinge.

CULTIVATION Galtonias should be planted about 15 cm deep in autumn and disturbed as little as possible. When growing in cooler districts, protect them from winter frost with a mulch. In very cold climates, lift and store over winter. Propagate by offsets or from seed.

Wide moisture and temperature range excluding tropical and dry inland conditions, are best.

PLANTING SEASON: Autumn.
FLOWERING SEASON: Summer.

GALTONIA

DIGGER'S GARDEN COMPANY

Gladiolus

(SWORD LILY, GLADIOLI, *IRIDACEAE*)

A genus of about two hundred species taking their name from their sword-like leaves (Latin for sword is 'gladius'). The most well known are the Large Flowered hybrids, which are now available in a vast range of colours from pure white to almost black. Many of the species are native of Europe, the Mediterranean region and tropical and South Africa. Gladioli are grown from corms, the compressed base of the stems, which produce two or three leaves and a usually one-sided spike of flowers.

Gladioli must have regular spray routines. Grown in clumps, they make a striking display in the garden and they are also extremely popular as cut flowers.

G. alatus has wide open fragrant flowers with winged petals, which are deep red with yellow-green at the base. Some lighter-coloured forms are

WHITE GLADIOLI

available; 30 cm. *G. byzantinus* (now *G. communis* subspecies *byzantinus*) flowers in late spring and has leaves about 30 cm long and the flower spike nearly three times as long. The flowers are red, or reddish-purple, with faint white markings. A white form is also available. Plant in late autumn, or, in cold climates, in very early spring; many cultivars are available.

G. x *colvillei*, a dwarf gladiolus, has given rise to many forms flowering in the late spring. The planting time is as for *G. byzantinus*. This species has given rise to a large number of hybrids. 'Insignis' is flame coloured, 60 cm. 'Nymph' is pale pink with distinct coral markings, 55 cm.

G. primulinus, flowering in summer, has yellow blooms, the tube curved to give a hooded effect. Parent of many hybrids; plant throughout spring.

G. tristis, which may be left undisturbed for some years, has slender foliage and short flower stems to 60 cm. Strongly perfumed flowers are pale yellow with dark purple marks on the upper petals. Spring flowering, it should be planted in late autumn.

CULTIVATION Gladioli must have full sun. They make splendid container subjects and the smaller growing sorts are ideal for that purpose. Very large, flattened corms can carry disease; buy them only from a reputable source.

Planting in the milder climatic areas is usual in July and August, later in the cooler areas, but a succession of plantings can be made, provided approximately fourteen weeks for flowering is allowed before first frost. In frost free areas, planting may take place at any time during the year providing flowers avoid extreme summer heat.

Bed preparation is necessary to ensure proper drainage. In heavy soils, which may be lightened by the addition of sand, it is sensible to build the bed up some 15 cm above normal soil level. Very acid soils will need a dressing of dolomite at the rate of 60–120 g per square metre.

Organic matter, such as compost or decayed cow manure may be added if

required, as well as commercial rose fertiliser or a home mixture of 600 g blood and bone, 900 g superphosphate and 100 g sulphate of potash. This mixture can be broadcast at 90 g per square metre and dug into the top 15–20 cm of soil. An alternative method is to make each planting hole wider and 3 cm deeper than the recommended depth. Sprinkle a level dessertspoon (3 teaspoons) of the mixture over the bottom and then cover it up with 3 cm of sand on which the corm is set.

Planting depths are 7–10 cm deep in heavy soils and 12–16 cm deep in sandy soils, the deeper planting is essential in light soils because of the top heavy nature of the flower spikes. Space corms in clumps, 15–20 cm apart, in rows, 15 cm apart with 45 cm between rows. For real impact, have several corms of the same variety together. When row planting, it is easier to dig a trench rather than separate holes. The depth should be the same as for separate holes, but the fertiliser should be run in a band. Cover the fertiliser with sand, set the corms in place on it and, as the huge flower spikes can be very top heavy, drive a stake in alongside each one. For tall sorts, a hardwood stake about 120 cm long is required.

Cover the corm with 3–4 cm of sand then fill in the rest of the hole or trench with soil. The sand is used as some infections can be soil-borne. When planting is completed, water the bed and mulch in hot dry weather. Keep the bed weeded and six weeks after planting, a side dressing of the same mixed fertiliser can be applied. Do not put it too close to the plants. For groups, use one level dessertspoonful (3 teaspoons) put in a ring 5 cm out from each plant, for rows use 40–50 g per metre, half on each side. Never overdo fertilisers. Water the bed after the side dressings have been applied and do not allow the bed to dry out at any time. Use a complete garden spray or an insecticide such as maldison regularly, once a week or at most every ten days, as insect pests can transmit virus diseases that may affect the corms so that they have to be destroyed.

When the plants are near full size and if windy weather prevails, it is wise to hill them up by throwing some additional soil around the main stems.

Flowers should be ready for picking in eleven to fourteen weeks after planting, though cold weather can slow down down. Flowers should be cut just as the second bud on the spike is starting to open. Using a sharp, pointed knife, cut the stem and draw it out, trying not to damage the leaves.

Once in a vase, the water should be changed every day and at the same time, a couple of centimetres snipped off the bottom of the stems.

After the flower spikes have been cut, continue to give the plant the usual care. When the foliage finally yellows and dies, dig the plants carefully and cut the remnants of the withered leaves back to within two centimetres of the new corm, which will have formed above the old one. The corms should be spread out on trays, baskets or sacking in a dry shed or garage. When quite dry, clean off the remains of the old corms, dust with derris or other insecticidal dust and store in paper bags, labelled with their colours.

Next planting season, the small cormlets which may be present around the base of the new corm, can be set out about 5 cm apart in a nursery bed, using the same soil type as for mature bulbs and giving the same care as flowering gladioli. The following year, the cormlets, after having been lifted and stored over winter, can be again planted in a nursery bed, this time spacing them about 10 cm apart. The next season, they will generally have reached flowering size and can be treated accordingly.

Cultural requirements supersede climatic conditions.

PLANTING SEASON: Late winter, spring, summer.

FLOWERING SEASON: Summer.

Hemerocallis

(DAY LILY, *LILIACEAE*)

A useful group of hardy, flowering perennials from Europe and Asia, whose cultivars are grown widely in temperate and subtropical areas. The individual blooms, usually borne in summer but sometimes throughout most of the year, are funnel-shaped and each lasts for only a day. However, as the flowers appear in clusters, a single head may be in bloom for weeks. Day lilies have been extensively hybridised and many cultivars are now available.

H. aurantiaca grows to 100 cm and produces clumps of characteristically long, narrow, pale green leaves. Flowers are orange-yellow and cultivars produce lemon, pink or purple flowers. *H. citrina* reaching just over 100 cm, has fragrant lemon yellow blooms. *H. fulva* has many cultivars, including *'Flore Pleno'*; to 100 cm with double, bright, rich orange flowers marked with dark brown.

H. x *luteola*, growing to 100 cm, has large, lemon coloured flowers standing up from dense clumps of foliage.

H. middendorffi, growing 30–45 cm, has sweetly scented, deep yellow flowers. *H. minor*, a dwarf species, reaches around 45 cm, with fragrant flowers, reddish-brown on the outside and yellow inside. *H. thunbergii*, growing to 100 cm, bears fragrant, bright yellow flowers. Many cultivars are available, producing flowers of red, apricot, soft pink, deep brown and purple.

Some of these include 'Bonanza', light orange with maroon centre; 'Morocco Red', maroon-red with a yellow throat; 'Pink Damask', warm pink with a yellow throat.

CULTIVATION Day lilies are fairly hardy but should be grown so that the flowers are naturally turned towards the light. Brightly coloured varieties should be planted in half-shade to prevent the flowers from fading. None of them, however, should be grown in full shade. Plant in autumn or spring after adding some manure or compost to the soil. Propagate by division of existing plants or grow from seed.

The climate is not critical.

PLANTING SEASON: Autumn to winter.

FLOWERING SEASON: Summer.

Hippeastrum

(HIPPEASTRUM FIRE LILY, AMARYLLIDACEAE)

Hippeastrum is often confused with the Belladonna Lily (*Amaryllis belladonna*) and was at one time included in the genus *Amaryllis*. Hippeastrum is a spring-flowering bulb, while the Belladonna Lily flowers in late summer and autumn. Both grow in warm climates.

HIPPEASTRUM

Like the *Amaryllis*, *Hippeastrum* bulbs are extremely large and must be planted with the neck of the bulb above soil level.

Leaves are strap-like, broad, green and glossy, appearing with or after the flowers.

The flowers are funnel-form, often extremely large with conspicuous protruding stamens and borne on thick hollow stems. The colour range is striking, with clear vivid reds, pinks, or white or mixtures, some with contrasting colours at the throat and some with broken stripes, or banded.

HEMEROCALLIS FULVA

H. aulicum, growing to 60 cm, has crimson and purple flowers with green throats. *H. pratense*, to 40 cm, has bright red or purple-violet flowers. *H. psittacinum* has striped orange and scarlet flowers. *H. puniceum*, Barbados Lily, to 45 cm, has bright red flowers with green base.

H. reginae, growing to 60 cm, has red and white flowers with greenish-white throats. *H. reticulatum*, to 30 cm, has bright reddish-mauve flowers with deeper markings.

H. striatum, also to 30 cm, has green and crimson flowers. Named hybrids are available in pure white, salmon, dark red and various colours in striped effects.

H. vittatum has broad leaves, green and strap-like to 45 cm long. Flowers are funnel-form to 10 cm across in clusters of 4–6 on long stout stems. Hybrids of many colours are available in clear reds, pinks, white and bi-colours, some with stripes or bands, or contrasting throat.

CULTIVATION The bulbs are fist-sized and are planted in winter. The neck of the bulb should be just above soil level, and there should be 25–30 cm between each bulb. Once established, they should be left undisturbed. Hippeastrum require heavy, rich, well drained soil and should be planted in a sunny position. Cultivars can be propagated from division of the bulbs or sown from seed.

Warm to hot moist coastal to tropical climatic areas.

PLANTING SEASON: Winter.
FLOWERING SEASON: Late spring.

Hyacinthus

(HYACINTH, *LILIACEAE*)

In Greek mythology, the god Apollo is said to have accidentally killed Hyakithos and the blood soaked earth where he died produced these beautiful flowering plants, now called Hyacinths. They are native to the Mediterranean area but are also found in Asia Minor, Syria and tropical and southern Africa, and have proven hardy survivors when introduced into Australian and New Zealand conditions. *Hyacinthus* is a bulbous, perennial genus originally of more than thirty species, but now greatly reduced owing to recent reclassification.

H. orientalis, Common Garden Hyacinth, originating in the eastern Mediterranean, grows 15–30 cm with very fragrant, funnel-shaped flowers of various colours in dense racemes. It is still cultivated as a source of perfume.

H. orientalis var. *albulus*, from which has been developed the Roman Hyacinth, has smaller, white or blue flowers. Cultivars of *H. orientalis* are available in white, pale blue, deep blue, pink, red and yellow flowers.

CULTIVATION Well drained soil, about 10 cm deep, with added bone meal, in a sunny situation, provides the best conditions. The bulbs should be planted in autumn about 20 cm apart. For winter blooms, bulbs are planted in pots in a porous soil and leaf mould or bulb fibre.

These should be kept in a cool, dark place for about eight weeks until the roots have formed; they can then be placed in a reasonably light position at about 18–21°C. After they have bloomed once, the bulbs can be planted out. Bulbs can also be grown in specially designed glass bowls in water. Propagation is by seed planted in light soil in boxes which should be kept in a cold frame. It takes three years for the seedlings to begin to flower. Hyacinths are also propagated by bulblets or offsets removed from the old bulbs. These are best planted in open beds in autumn and take two to three years to bloom.

Basal Cuttings: Hyacinths are most commonly increased by these methods of cutting into the base plate of the bulbs — scooping, scoring and coring.

The bulb to be treated must be of a large, fully-matured size in each case, lifted when the leaves have died down completely.

Scooping: A sharp-edged spoon or small, razor-edged knife is used to scoop cut the whole basal plate. The cut should be deep enough to remove the main shoot. Small bulblets will develop from the wounded tissue at the base of the bulb scales. This method may produce about 20 new bulblets.

Scoring: Make straight knife cuts either in a V-shape or in three straight cuts right across the basal plate. Each cut must be deep enough to go through the basal plate and the growing point. Bulblets will grow along the cuts.

Coring: Use a sharp, domestic apple corer and press down firmly through the centre of the bulb around the growing point. Again bulblets will grow from the cut section of the basal plate.

All tools must be disinfected before each cut by dipping in a five percent solution of household bleach or in other household disinfectant.

The wounded bulb should be set aside in a dry, shady spot to dry the wounded area completely before planting. Plant in a freely draining, sandy loam and do not overwater.

The mother bulbs can be planted in nursery beds or containers until the next season. Usually the mother bulb will disintegrate leaving a mass of bulblets which should be replaced in enriched soil until they grow to flowering size — this may take several years. Yearly lifting and replanting in renovated soil helps to hasten the process.

Moist, cool coastal and high climatic areas.

PLANTING SEASON: Autumn.
FLOWERING SEASON: Spring.

HYACINTHUS ORIENTALIS

Ipheion

(SPRING STAR FLOWER, *AMARYLLIDACEAE*)

Introduced to Europe from Peru in the 19th century, this genus of low growing, bulbous plants comprises some twenty-five species. Growing to less than 30 cm, they produce stems of bluish-white flowers from among their grassy leaves. They flower in late spring; the foliage then dies down during summer to reappear in autumn, and lies on the ground during winter. The blossoms, in the shape of a six-petalled star, have a mint-like scent, but the leaves, when crushed, smell like onion.

I. uniflorum (syn. *Brodiaea uniflora*, *Milla uniflora* and *Triteleia uniflora*), Spring Starflower, is the only species known in cultivation. This tiny bulb is suitable in beds, borders, rockeries, naturalised plantings or in a container. The blossoms are 2–5 cm across and bluish-white.

CULTIVATION Ipheions will grow in full sun or partial shade and prefer a milder winter climate where temperatures do not fall below −10°C. Plant bulbs in late summer or early autumn, 15 cm apart and covered with 8 cm of soil. They do not require fertiliser and the bulbs will multiply quickly. These can be divided in midsummer every few years. Also successful as indoor plants, they require at least four hours of direct sunlight. They should be potted in a light mixture about 3 cm deep. The potting mix should be kept moist during the growing and flowering season, until the foliage dies down in summer. The bulbs should then be lifted, stored in a dry area, and separated for repotting in autumn.

Most climatic conditions except hot tropics are suitable.

PLANTING SEASON: Late summer to early autumn.

FLOWERING SEASON: Late spring.

IPHEION UNIFLORUM

Iris

(RAINBOW FLOWER, *IRIDACEAE*)

The iris, or Rainbow Flower, is truly well named. References to this flower have appeared in religion, myths, legends, in medicine and botany, and in the fields of heraldry and magic. Well known favourites such as babianas, sparaxis, watsonias and gladioli are members of the *Iridaceae* family, which includes hundreds of species.

Irises are essentially northern hemisphere plants, but there are members of the family *Iridaceae,* such as *Patersonia*, indigenous to the southern hemisphere. The dark bluish-purple flowers of *Patersonia* are short-lived but come in profusion from late spring to summer. Propagation is from seed but supply is not readily available.

In attempting to classify the iris family it is probably simplest to consider separately the bearded and beardless species.

BEARDED IRISES The general flower form of the iris is one of six petals in two sets of three. In the bearded iris, there are three upright petals called standards and three nearly horizontal petals called falls. These falls are adorned with bushy appendages called beards which serve no biological function other than the possible attraction of potential natural pollinators.

Aril Irises and *Arilbreds:* These are among the first bearded irises to flower in the season. Native to the Middle East, they are not readily available, due to difficulty in cultivation, but in suitable conditions present a spectacular display of bizarre colour patterns. Cultivar 'Aphrodite of Melos', light lavender, brown and black; 'Jade', green with blue flecks and brown markings; 'Mehetabel', dark purple standards, red-black falls, white and copper markings around black-purple beards.

Dwarf Bearded Irises: The miniatures grow from 12–25 cm, and the standards from 25–35 cm, are also early flowerers, presenting a blaze of colour in spring. Because of their size

and growing habits, they are ideal for the rock garden. Cultivar 'Chanted', smoky mid-pink, strong lavender blue beards; 'Doodle', purple and white flowers; 'Buzz Me', lemon yellow standards, white surrounded lavender beards.

Intermediate Irises: These vary in height from 38–70 cm and have larger flowers than the dwarfs. Cultivar 'Tchin-tchin', peach standards, falls lighter, orange beards; 'Cheers', white flowers with a blue beard; 'Sinbad the Sailor', gold and brown flowers.

Tall Bearded Irises: When in bloom they are the highlight of the iris season. If a selection of early, mid season and late cultivars is made, magnificent flowers will bloom from spring to early summer. They are useful cut flowers, as each spike will present a continuous display for a week or more.

Cultivars include white, yellow, blue, violet, purple, black, red, brown, orange, pink and even some green flowers with contrasting or matching beards, some blooms veined with contrasting colours.

Cultivar 'Going My Way', white ground, purple plicata; 'Osage Buff', apricot ground, garnet red plicata; 'Decolletage', cream ground, mulberry plicata. Bicolour Tall Bearded Irises have different colours or shades of colour in the standards from those in the falls. Cultivar 'Precious Moments', creamy yellow standards, white falls; 'In Tempo', pink standards, purplish-black falls; 'English Charm', cream standards, veined yellow, light apricot falls, tangerine beards; 'Outer Limits', white standards, blue falls and red beards.

Border Bearded Irises: These are plants from tall iris breeding which do not reach 70 cm; they are useful for planting in front of the taller varieties. Cultivar 'Doll Baby', wattled deep rich pink flowers; 'Royal Ruffles', beautiful, royal blue flowers.

CULTIVATION Aril Irises require sharp drainage, hot, dry summers and cold winters for successful cultivation. Not easy to grow, they are difficult to obtain, but arilbred iris, are more easily grown and

more readily available. Dwarf Irises also need a cold winter to flower well. They demand efficient drainage, fertile soil and full sun and won't grow successfuly in mild, humid, coastal regions. Intermediate Irises require similar cultivation but some will grow well where dwarfs fail.

Tall and Border Bearded Irises need sharp drainage, a well composted, heavily fertilised soil and maximum sunlight. They prefer a cold winter but take a milder winter better than Dwarf Irises. Rhizomes should be planted, or old clumps divided, from December through to April in prepared soil, and then well watered until established. Best results are obtained by adding a fertiliser of approximately 5:5:10 composition or by using Osmocote, preferably the eight to nine month type, at planting time. The rhizomes should be planted at ground level. In early spring they should be given a further feeding and watered well. At least one flowering spike should be obtained in the first season. Once a rhizome has flowered it will not flower again, but should give from two to six or more increases which mature and flower the following year. Well cultivated irises will produce clumps with a dozen or more spikes in three to four years, after which, divide the clumps and replant the best rhizomes.

New and often exciting cultivars can be obtained from seed by intercrossing the Iris. Pollen from the anthers of one iris is taken and rubbed across the stigmatic lip of another. The pods ripen in six to eight weeks, whereupon they first lighten in colour, then turn brown and split at the top. Once the pod has turned brown the seed can be harvested, allowed to dry for about four to six weeks, and then planted. The new seedlings will appear in the autumn and the first flowers are obtained two years after the initial cross.

Bearded Irises are relatively disease and pest free. Rhizome rot can be a problem with some cultivars in humid areas. If rot occurs, the infected section should be scraped clean and the rhizome left to dry. Leaf spot can be controlled with most of the available fungicides. Aphids can also be a nuisance unless they are washed off frequently with a hose or sprayed with an insecticide such as maldison.

IRIS 'DISTRACTION'

IRIS 'SEA VENTURE'

BEARDLESS IRISES This category can be further divided into three groups: Bulbous Irises, Crested Irises and Smooth-falled Rhizomatous Irises.

Bulbous Irises: These are, for the most part, cold climate flowers; the small but beautiful landscape specimens such as *I. histrioides* and *I. reticulata* and their hybrids are rapid to increase and attractive in clumps and drifts. Dutch iris cultivars include: 'Bronze Queen', flowers with bronze tonings; 'Professor Blaauw', dark blue flowers; 'Golden Harvest', yellow flowers.

CULTIVATION *I. reticulata*, *I. histrioides* and their hybrids need efficient drainage, a cold winter and minimum humid heat and hot dry summer period to flower to satisfaction. They are otherwise undemanding in their culture. Bulbs are usually available in late summer, should be planted in autumn, and flower in early spring. As soon as the foliage dies down they can be lifted and stored for planting the following season. English irises require much the same culture, while Spanish and Dutch irises will thrive in somewhat milder climates and withstand humid summer conditions.

Dutch irises flower in late spring. Bulbs should be purchased from reputable nursery people as many are virus infected and the weakened bulb will gradually be lost, while the infected foliage is unattractive; however, this seems to be the only problem in growing these irises.

Crested Irises: Evansias or crested iris are distinguished from other types by the raised crest on the falls. *I. japonica*, blooming in September and October, has 3 cm, light blue flowers with yellow signal markings and fimbriated crests, borne on multi-branched stems holding thirty or more buds which open in succession and last two days. The variegated leaf form is equally easy to grow but shy to bloom. *I. tectorum*, Japanese Roof Iris, so called because it is grown on the thatched roofs of Japanese houses, is actually a native of China. There are two distinct colour forms, a bluish-violet and a white. *I unguicularis* (syn. *I. stylosa*) a small, winter flowering, beardless iris, is undemanding in culture and useful in

IRIS SIBIRICA

providing flowers in white and varying shades of blue when there is less colour in the garden. The thin reedy foliage is a favourite haunt for snails so bait needs to be put down, and it is advisable to cut down the foliage in autumn as these irises flower among the foliage and can remain unobserved. *I. wattii*, similar to *I. japonica*, has larger mid-blue flowers, but fewer on the spike. Cultivar 'Darjeeling', light blue flowers.

CULTIVATION Easily grown from rhizome division or from seed, all evansias prefer a semi-shaded position in the garden and grow best in a well fertilised, medium soil which will ensure rapid increase and prolific flowering. *I. Wattii* is subtropical and suits warm, summer rainfall areas. *I. tectorum* takes a few degrees of frost (to -5˚C) and should be planted in a protected, semi-shaded position in colder areas. It should be moved after two to three years.

Smooth-Falled Rhizomatous Irises: Californian or Pacific Coast Irises form a group made up of several species and hybrids developed by intercrossing these species. Generally low growing iris, they are ideal for rockeries and borders as they quickly form large clumps which come into bloom in late spring and flower through a couple of months. The flowers average 5–8 cm in diameter and come in a wide range of colours and patterns.

Spuria Irises produce orchid-like flowers on long stems late in spring. Their tall, upright foliage provides an accent in the garden, dying down after flowering but shooting again in late summer. Cultivar 'Destination', bright deep orange flowers; 'Minneopa' and 'One Reason', yellow, blue and white flowers; 'Mystifier', lemon yellow standards, deeper gold falls.

Louisiana Irises, native to the swamps of southern North America, have a complete colour range and while clumps in full bloom are a most beautiful sight, their major attraction is as cut flowers. Cultivar 'Charlie's Felicia', light and dark violet flowers; 'Top Start', blue to violet bitone, yellow signal, heavily ruffled; 'Ira S. Nelson', rose red blooms with yellow signals on all petals; 'White Umbrella', large white flowers with green-gold veins, lightly ruffled .

I. pseudacorus, Yellow Flag or English Wild Iris, like the Louisiana Iris, stays green and attractive through winter. A tall reed-like water edging plant to 100 cm, it has bright yellow flowers in spring.

Siberian Irises, which should be left in the same position for some years, flower in late spring to early summer. The attractive flowers are mainly in blue and purple tonings. Cultivar 'Ego', violet blue flowers; 'Halcyon Seas', dark blue-purple flowers;

'Turquoise Cup', turquoise blooms; 'Anniversary', white flowers.

Japanese Irises (*Iris ensata* syn. *I. Kaempferi*) bring the season to a spectacular conclusion with their large 30 cm flowers with horizontal petals. The cultivars come in a wide range of colours with stripes and fleckings and frilled and fluted edges. Cultivar 'Banners on Parade', six petals, purple and white; 'Hagoromo', nine petals, superb pure white flowers, sometimes with irregular lavender markings; 'Nishiki-Gi', six petals, multicoloured, speckled blue, purple and magenta on white; 'Peacock Dance', three petals, charming white and violet flowers.

CULTIVATION Californian Irises need a rich soil and a position protected from the hot afternoon sun in summer for best results. Drainage should be efficient and clumps should be left undisturbed for several years. They are very difficult to transplant. The most suitable means of propagation is from seed which is easy to set and germinate.

Spuria Irises are also reasonably easy to cultivate but difficult to transplant. For this reason, they should be planted in their permanent position. They like a rich soil with plenty of water in the growing season which differs from that of other irises; after flowering, they remain dormant during summer and the foliage shoots again in winter. Dwarf species will not tolerate humidity.

Adaptability is a key word in describing Louisiana Irises because they can be grown in shade, part shade or full sun; they will grow beautifully in standing water, in bog conditions and in the normal garden setting in most soils. Like most beardless irises, they prefer an acid soil that has been liberally composted and well fertilised.

Siberian Irises are easy to cultivate but should be planted in a permanent position. Planting can be done in autumn or winter as the foliage dies right down during the colder months. Liking plenty of water in the growing season, they flower best in climates with cold winters.

Japanese Irises need great quantities of water during the growing season which commences in spring after they have been dormant during autumn and winter. Planting in the open ground or pots is best done in this dormant period and the soil needs adequate preparation with humus and a fertiliser such as Osmocote. They are very suitable for pot cultivation as the pot can be placed in standing water during the growing season and then removed during the dormant period when the plants need only ordinary watering.

PLANTING SEASON: Bearded Irises in late summer to autumn; Dutch, English and Spanish Irises in autumn.

FLOWERING SEASON: Bearded Irises in late spring; Dutch, English and Spanish Irises in spring.

TIM SIMPSON

IRIS

Ixia

(AFRICAN CORN LILY, IRIDACEAE)

Comprising about 60 species of cormous plants with very sticky sap, this genus is native to the Cape Province of South Africa. Growing to about 50 cm, they bear bright, scented, spring to early summer flowers, about 5 cm across. Colours include red, pink, orange, yellow and cream, and most have dark centres. The blossoms open fully to a flat position only in sunshine, forming an attractive cup shape when partly open. The narrow linear foliage dies down to the ground in midsummer. Most attractive planted in massed groups in the garden, they also make good house plants and cut flowers.

I. campanulata (syn. *I. speciosa*) growing to 30–45 cm, has purple to dark crimson flowers in spring. *I. maculata*, growing to 60 cm, has orange yellow flowers in spring, with purple-black eyes. *I. patens*, reaching about 45 cm, has pink spring flowers with green throats. *I. viridiflora*, growing to 30 cm, has pale, bluish-green, dark throated flowers in spring.

Ixia hybrids are derived from crossing *I. maculata*, *I. monadelpha*, *I. paniculata*, and *I. campanulata*. They come in a wide range of vibrant colours in red, pink, lilac, blue, yellow, orange, cream, white, usually with a dark base. They flower in spring, 45–100 cm.

CULTIVATION Ixias are hardy but prefer a moderate climate. Set the corms 5–8 cm deep in the open with a little sand sprinkled under them. They will usually stand being left in the ground for some years but can be lifted each year and replanted in the spring. Propagate by removing the small corms that develop beside the large ones. Ixias may also be started from seeds but they will take about three years to reach flowering size.

Most climatic conditions excluding hot tropical; also dry inland and warmer high areas.

PLANTING SEASON: Autumn.
FLOWERING SEASON: Spring.

IXIA VIRIDIFLORA

RED-HOT POKER, KNIPHOFIA UVARIA

Kniphofia

(TORCH LILY, RED HOT POKER, LILIACEAE)

These striking, erect plants from South Africa bear strap-shaped leaves and long-lasting, poker-like heads of many small flowers. They will add style and colour to background and border positions and in groups with shrubs.

K. caulescens, growing to 120 cm, has rosettes of long leaves on a woody stem and dense, 15 cm long spikes of flowers that turn red to greenish yellow. *K. foliosa*, with 100 cm long, sword-shaped leaves and bright yellow flowers forming 30 cm spikes, is from Ethiopia and grows to 100 cm. *K. triangularis* (syn. *K. galpinii*), a slender plant of 60–100 cm, has reddish-orange flowers in racemes to 8 cm long. *K. macowanii*, growing to 60 cm, has 10 cm spikes of yellow to vivid orange-red flowers. *K. northiae*, recognised by its very long, bluish leaves which sometimes reach 150 cm, grows to 120 cm and bears 30 cm spikes of red flowers which become yellow with age. *K. pumila*, growing to 60 cm, has orange flowers and bluish foliage. *K. uvaria*, the most popular species, has coral red flowers and grows 60–200 cm tall. Many cultivars giving various flower colours are available.

CULTIVATION Kniphofias are adaptable to almost any garden soil, but prefer a light, well drained soil. They grow best in full sun but should be watered well in hot weather. Propagation is by seed, the new plants taking up to three years to flower, or by division of the cord-like roots in spring.

Most conditions except hot tropics. More temperate high areas are preferred. Some cultivars are fully cold hardy. Others will only take a few degrees of frost.

PLANTING SEASON: Spring.
FLOWERING SEASON: Summer, autumn or winter depending on cultivar.

Lachenalia

(SOLDIER BOY, CAPE COWSLIP, *LILIACEAE*)

Lachenalias are small bulb plants related to lilies, and are native to South Africa. The name honours an 18th century botanist, Professor M. de la Chenal. The flowers are upright spikes containing small white, yellow or red tubular flowers and the lily-like leaves are sometimes spotted at the base. Mass-planted, these bright flowers make a wonderful spring display. They are very hardy and, because of their small size, are especially suitable for borders and rockeries. The flowers tend to retain colour even after drying, and make good cut blooms. Lachenalias may be grown in pots or baskets.

L. aloides, growing to 30 cm, with leaves sometimes spotted, has flower spikes with drooping yellow, red-tipped bells.

Cultivar 'Aurea', orange based golden yellow flowers; 'Conspicua', orange flowers with purple veins and yellowish tips; 'Luteola', lemon flowers with green tips; 'Nelson', yellow flowers with green tinges; 'Quadricolor', red flowers merging to greenish, tips green, inside bells purple to green.

L. bachmanni, growing to 25 cm, has red flowers with white tips. *L. bulbifera*, a hardy species to 25 cm, has orange flowers, purple inside. *L. glaucina*, growing to 40 cm, has unusual iridescent flowers of glowing red, yellow and blue with green flashes. *L. juncifolia*, a small species, has red-tinged white flowers. *L. liliflora*, growing to 30 cm, has white cylindrical flowers. *L. mutabilis*, with blue and green flowers turning brown with age, grows to 30 cm. *L. orchioides*, growing to 40 cm, has spotty leaves, and flowers variable from blue-green, to pink, white or yellow.

CULTIVATION Lachenalias are hardy and like full sun. They will grow in any well drained garden loam, and respond to fertiliser. Plant bulbs in masses for best results, in autumn, approximately 5–6 cm deep. They can be clumped, or planted in pockets of rockeries. In pots, plant up to five in a good potting mix with sharp drainage. These plants flower over a long period, and cut blooms will last well although the stems bend in water. Lachenalias are bird-attracting plants and are relatively free from pests and disease. Propagate from seed, or by division of bulbs after flowering.

Cool to warm temperate and mild inland climatic areas. In cold climates can be grown in pots.

PLANTING SEASON: Autumn.
FLOWERING SEASON: Winter, spring.

LACHENALIA 'TRICOLOUR'

Leucojum

(SNOWFLAKE, AMARYLLIDACEAE)

A small genus of herbaceous bulbous plants whose flowers resemble large snowdrops, *Leucojum* species are native to central Europe and the Mediterranean region.

L. aestivum, Summer Snowflake, from southern Europe, has white flowers tipped with green.

L. autumnale, Autumn Snowflake, growing to 15 cm, has white autumn flowers tinted with pink. The leaves develop after the flowers.

L. vernum, Spring Snowflake from central Europe, with white flowers tipped with green, grows to 30 cm.

CULTIVATION The bulbs should be planted to a depth of 8 cm and left undisturbed for some years. They like deep, well drained soil and a situation in semi-shade. The bulbs of the autumn flowering species should be planted out in mid-summer and those of the spring and early summering flowering species should be planted in autumn.

Most climatic conditions except hot subtropical and tropical areas are suitable.

PLANTING SEASON: Early summer for autumn species, autumn for spring-flowering species.

FLOWERING SEASON: Winter, spring, autumn.

LEUCOJUM VERNUM

Lilium

(LILIACEAE)

According to historians, the first illustrations of liliums were on Cretan pottery about 2000 BC and bulbs were found in mummy cases in Egypt, no doubt placed there for the spirit of the departed, as the bulbs were used for food and medicinal purposes. The earliest known type is the Madonna Lily (*L. candidum*), a native to the Mediterranean basin and long used as a symbol of purity, white *L. chalcedonicum* is considered by some to be the scarlet lily of the fields mentioned in the Bible.

LILIUM AURATUM 'CRIMSON QUEEN'

LILIUM

The genus *Lilium*, containing the true lilies as opposed to day or arum lilies, is distinguished by the fleshy scales of the bulbs which are not enclosed by an outer protective skin or membrane. The flower spike has stem-clasping leaves, which have parallel veins and are flat and not rolled when young. The terminal flowers are on stalks, which have a small leaf attached where they join the main stem. Normal flowers have three sepals, three petals and six anthers on slender stamens. In the centre of the flower the embryo seed pod is joined by the style to the rounded, three-lobed stigma. The nectar is secreted from a furrow at the base of the petals. The seed pod contains three compartments, which split from the top down the sides, allowing the thin, flat seeds to scatter in the breeze.

Most of the easily available lilies are hybrids.

L. auratum, Golden-rayed Lily, is from Japan. The large, white, heavily scented flowers have golden bands running from throat to petal edge and are spotted with purplish-red flecks. The tall stems, 100–275 cm high, bear twenty or more flowers. *L. candidum*, Madonna Lily, has glistening, pure white, trumpet-shaped flowers in

November. One of the earliest recorded species, it is not the easiest to grow. *L. henryi*, has vigorous growth, and small, drooping, reflexed, orange flowers. *L. longiflorum*, Christmas Lily, a hardy, vigorous grower with white, trumpet-shaped flowers, is used extensively for garden landscapes, cut flowers and church decoration. *L. regale*, a popular species, has trumpet-shaped flowers, rose-purple on the outside with a throat of white blending to yellow; the large flower heads are extremely useful for garden display. *L. rubellum*, an early flowering oriental, grows to 50 cm tall and bears clear, glowing pink flowers. This species has been used extensively in hybridising.

Lilium cultivars include Atomic hybrids, (*L. auratum* x *L. rubellum* from *L. japonicum* hybrids), which have beautiful white to pink flowers from November to February. 'Chinook', an outstanding Asiatic of Canadian origin, has creamy apricot, upfacing flowers; used for both the garden and cutting. 'La Petite', miniature 'Oriental' suited to pot culture, grows to 60 cm tall, with ornamental foliage and carrying up to fourteen, white flowers. 'Red Carpet', a low growing Asiatic suitable for rock gardens and containers with large, upfacing flowers is velvety red. 'Pirate', an attractively shaped plant with bright red flowers with orange flush at the centres.

CULTIVATION Most liliums will grow in acid or slightly alkaline soil, but they all need effective drainage, sunshine and shade in equal amounts, and a cool root run; late varieties need additional shade as they flower when the sun is at its hottest. If the ground selected for the bulbs has been well manured for a previous crop, further fertilisation is usually unnecessary. Otherwise, a generous amount of properly made compost, with the addition of a handful of complete fertiliser to each square metre, would be beneficial. For pot culture, a mixture of two parts loam, two parts peat, one part coarse sand and one part styrene foam or verniculite will ensure a well drained and crumbly mixture. When mixing the

components, add to each 4 litres one teaspoon of complete fertiliser or slow release fertiliser to ensure the plant is well nourished when in growth.

At no time must lilium bulbs be allowed to dry out, so it is wise to check their condition before purchasing. Before planting, put them in a mesh bag and hose thoroughly. Dark brown diseased scales must be removed. The number of potential plants can be increased by taking, with the aid of a sharp knife, a couple of healthy scales from the outside of the bulb close to the base; put them back in the mesh bag. Prepare a dip of one teaspoon of a systemic fungicide, such as Benlate and one teaspoon of insecticide, such as maldison, in an 8 litre bucket of water, stir thoroughly then hang the mesh bag in the mixture for thirty minutes. Hang the bag in a shady spot till dry; the bulbs are then ready for planting, free of insects and fungi spores.

Except for *L. candidum*, which must be planted with the top near the surface of the soil, cover the bulbs with 7–10 cm of soil with a little more for extra large bulbs. After planting, give the bulbs a thorough soaking to settle the soil around them. During the growing season, plenty of water must be supplied and this emphasises the need for efficient drainage. When watering, put a 7 cm deep tin on the bed and start the sprinkler. When the tin is full, the bed will have been watered sufficiently and it will not be necessary to water again for a week. This method is much better than a daily sprinkle which only produces sappy growth unable to withstand a dry period. In pot culture, a close watch must be maintained, as about two days is sufficient to dry the bulbs out, unless in a very sheltered position.

Bulbs may be left for years in one spot in the garden, provided care is taken to keep the ground cool in the heat and sufficient nourishment is made available. Even rich, volcanic soil needs plenty of organic matter added to it periodically. Deficiencies often show at flowering time by yellowing of the leaves from the base. Magnesium and potash are the usual elements needed, and these may be supplied by adding half a teaspoon of Epsom salts and half a teaspoon of sulphate of potash to 8 litres

water; apply by lightly watering over the foliage once a week, from the time the buds show until the time the flowers open.

Several methods of propagation exist. If left alone, bulbs will naturally divide, forming two and sometimes more bulbs. In some species, stem bulbs will form at the base of the stem, above the bulbs but under the ground. When these are removed at the end of the growing season and planted individually, they will usually grow and occasionally produce a single bloom at the next flowering season. Some Liliums form bulbils in the leaf axils; when they are ready to fall they may be removed and planted in seedling trays in autumn. Flowering should occur in two years. Propagation by scales taken from the bulbs (usually only from the two outer layers) is another method. Once removed from the bulb after washing, and after soaking in the fungicide-insecticide solution, the scales can be put in a plastic bag containing damp peat from which the water has been squeezed then loosened so that there is air for the developing bulblets. Tie the top of the bag to keep the moisture in and put in a warm dark spot (26°C is ideal). In three weeks small bulblets may be removed from the scales and treated as small plants.

Another inexpensive method of obtaining Liliums is to raise them from seed, obtainable from Lilium societies or the most recent flowering crop. In hybridising, the seed parent must have the anthers, containing the pollen, removed before it sheds; when the stigma (female organ) becomes moist and shiny, pollen from the desired male parent must be liberally sprinkled on the surface of the stigma. In a short time, the flower will fade and the seed pod will assume an upright position. Be sure to label the pod, noting both the parents used and the date, for later reference. Seed may be planted in March or August in the same potting mix as already mentioned. Loosely fill the seed tray with the mixture, making sure it is damp, sow the seed then firm it down to bring it into close contact with the soil. A mulch is then sprinkled over the seed to help retain moisture, and may consist of any material that will not cake, such as vermiculite or well rotted cow manure. If peat is to be used,

LILIUM 'JILLIAN WALLACE'

water by immersing the tray. Asiatic (epigeal) types or those that send up a leaf on germination, appear in about three weeks. Oriental (hypogeal) varieties which form a bulblet before showing the first leaf, if sown in autumn, will show the first leaf in spring. To obtain the same result, seed may be sown in damp peat in a plastic bag kept in a warm situation; on germination, the bulblet is transferred to the food storage compartment of the refrigerator for six weeks, before sowing in the seed tray in the usual manner. The first leaf will show in a short time. Asiatic seedlings will usually flower in two years; Oriental ones in three years.

The worst pests of liliums are slugs, snails and aphids. In spring, if pellets are scattered every three weeks, especially after rain, they will be kept under control. While spraying for aphids in spring and autumn it is as well to add a fungicide. You can buy combined sprays containing fungicides and insecticides. Choose the least toxic one. Observe all precautions recommended by the manufacturer when using any sprays.

Most climatic conditions are suitable, except hot tropics.

PLANTING SEASON: Late autumn to winter.

FLOWERING SEASON: Summer.

Lycoris

(SPIDER LILY, AMARYLLIDACEAE)

An attractive genus of some 18 species of bulbous flowering plants, natives of Japan and China, the species are noted for their funnel-shaped flowers which can be red, pink, white or yellow.

Lycoris have narrow, strap-like leaves and in some species these leaves have a narrow, grey-green stripe in the centre, from base to top. They are true tunicated bulbs.

Spider Lilies come from environments where drainage is sharp and where the hot dry summers prepare the bulbs for flowering in the autumn so that, like most bulbs of this type, they should be planted with the apex or neck of the bulb just above soil level.

The flowers appear before the leaves on stout stalks up to 30 cm long. The beautifully recurved segments, some almost curling back to the stem, are fluted or ruffled on their edges, and both have the pronounced curving stamens which give the plants their common name.

ORIENTAL SPIDER LILY, *LYCORIS RADIATA*

L. aureata (syn *L. africana*), Golden Spider Lily, growing to 40 cm, has delightful yellow flowers. Suitable for warm districts only. *L. radiata*, Japanese Spider Lily, has vivid scarlet flowers, with many stamens. It grows well in protected sea coast gardens. *L. sanguinea*, growing to 60 cm, has red flowers in summer. *L. squamigera*, Resurrection Lily, with lilac pink summer flowers, grows to 60 cm.

CULTIVATION Plants need sunny warm, sheltered conditions, and a hot dry summer resting period. In cool areas, plants are best grown in pots in a glassed-in sunroom or glasshouse. They prefer a light, well drained soil and only moderate watering while in flower.

The Spider Lily will grow in any average garden soil as long as it is well drained. Weeds must be kept down and moisture conserved by an organic mulch, which should not be placed closer than 2.5 cm from the edge of the clump. They will grow in subtropical gardens, providing they have plenty of room around them, and in coastal gardens with some protection from salt spray. Spider Lilies resent disturbance and appear to flower better when crowded for a number of years. Hot, well drained rock pockets suit them, but they should be placed where their delicate beauty is not obscured by other plants. They grow well in tubs or large pots where they can colonise, and then be moved into a warm and prominent position when they commence to flower. Propagation is by offsets from the mother bulb, although some species set seed freely enough to use this method.

Wet subtropics to tropical coastal areas are the best climatic conditions.

PLANTING SEASON: Summer when bulbs are dormant.

FLOWERING SEASON: Late summer, autumn.

MUSCARI ARMENIACUM, GRAPE HYACINTH

Muscari

(GRAPE HYACINTH, *LILIACEAE*)

The name is derived from the Greek word 'moschos', musk, in reference to the slight musk scent of some species. *Muscari* is a genus of about fifty species of bulbous, herbaceous, perennial, spring-flowering plants native to the Mediterranean and south-western Asia. The spikes of small, rounded, bell-shaped flowers rise out of the rushlike foliage and are attractive when massed as a garden border. Colours range from sky blue to lavender blue, but a few species carry yellow flowers.

M. armeniacum, growing to 23 cm, has deep violet flowers, less rounded and longer than other species; cultivars available such as paler lilac blue 'Blue Spike'. *M. azureum*, growing 15–20 cm, has tubular, bright blue flowers.

Cultivar 'Album' has white flowers.

M. comosum, Tassel Grape Hyacinth, grows to 30 cm with some greenish-brown, lower, fertile flowers surmounted by many smaller, purplish-blue flowers.

Cultivar 'Plumosum' (syn. 'Monstrosum'), Feather Hyacinth, has sterile, violet flowers with deeply shredded feather petals and basal green leaves.

M. elegans has rounded, violet-blue flowers. *M. macrocarpum*, growing to 25 cm, has yellow flowers with purple lobes. *M. neglectum*, growing to 15 cm, has fragrant, dark blue flowers. *M. Botryoides*, 15-20 cm, has pale mid-blue flowers with white rim; there is a scented white form.

CULTIVATION *Muscari* species will grow in almost any position, but prefer a medium loam and semi-shade in warmer areas. The bulbs should be planted no later than March. They increase very rapidly and should be lifted and replanted periodically to avoid overcrowding.

Wide moisture and temperature range excluding tropical and dry inland climatic conditions.

PLANTING SEASON: Autumn.
FLOWERING SEASON: Spring.

Narcissus

(DAFFODIL AND JONQUIL, AMARYLLIDACEAE)

According to Greek legend, Narcissus was a beautiful youth who fell in love with his own reflection in the mirror-like waters of a crystal clear spring, pined away and died. From the earth where his body lay, there sprang up a lovely nodding flower — the *Narcissus*. The name 'daffodil' is alleged to have developed from an old English word meaning that which cometh early. Poets and playwrights referred to the plant as 'daffadowndilly'. *Narcissus* are tunicated bulbs native to the northern hemisphere.

Daffodils have one flower per stem; jonquils have several flowers per stem. The flowers are composed of a tube spreading into a wheel or circle of six, petal-like segments, or perianth, supporting a cup or the corona. The cup can be long and trumpet-shaped with flared edges, small and chalice-like, or simply a thin ring. After the flowers fade, the leaves often become large and begin to manufacture food. Thus the green foliage should never be cut down until it withers away naturally and the plant goes into dormancy.

Although yellow is the colour most associated with daffodils, this is no longer the only shade. Bi-coloured flowers have cups of pink or deep orange to nearly red, pure white or faintly tinted on the mouth. There are more than 40 known species and thousands of cultivars.

The Royal Horticultural Society devised a classification system dividing the types into eleven groups, many of which are further subdivided.

Trumpet Narcissi: Distinguishing characters are one flower to a stem, a trumpet or corona as long as, or longer than, the perianth segments. Four subdivisions cover colour variations. Cultivars, 'King Alfred' and 'Mount Hood' are included in the trumpets.

Large-cupped Narcissi: Distinguishing characters are one flower to a stem and cup or corona more than one third, but less than equal to, the length of the perianth segments. Four subdivisions cover colour variations. 'Carlton' and 'Fortune' are typical cultivars.

Small-cupped Narcissi. Distinguishing characters are one flower to a stem, a cup or corona not more than one third the length of the perianth segments. Four subdivisions exist, according to flower colour. Cultivars include 'Ice Follies' and 'Apricot Attraction'.

Double Narcissi: Distinguished by their double flowers, they include 'Golden Ducat' and 'White Lion'.

Triandrus Narcissi: Possessing the characteristics of *Narcissus triandrus*, cultivars of this division have one to about six flowers to a stem. Each bloom has a slender tube to 25 mm, fully reflexed, perianth segments of nearly the same length, and a small, cup-shaped corona about half the length of the perianth segments. Two subdivisions detail flower colour. Cultivars in the group include 'Thalia', 'Hawera' and 'Liberty Bells'.

Cyclamineus Narcissi: The characteristics of *Narcissus cyclamineus* are clearly evident: the one to three flowers to a stem are drooping, with short tube, fully reflexed, narrow, perianth segments about 25 mm long and a tubular corona of the same length with a frilly-edged mouth. Two subdivisions also exist, and cultivars in the group include 'February Gold' and 'Peeping Tom'.

Jonquilla Narcissi: Possessing the characteristics of *Narcissus jonquilla*, these cultivars have two to about six flowers to a stem consisting of a very slender tube about 25 mm long, perianth segments shorter, the corona a small cup about 6 mm long with a frilled edge. All are highly scented and two subdivisions exist. Examples of cultivars are 'Golden Sceptre' and 'Lanarth'.

Tazetta Narcissi: Distinguishing characteristics are those of *Narcissus tazetta*. The four to ten perfumed flowers to a stem consist of a greenish tube about 18 mm long and a cup-shaped corona about 6 mm long. One example is 'Cheerfulness'.

Poeticus Narcissi: This division includes those plants with the characteristics of *Narcissus poeticus* without admixture of any other species. Flowers are solitary and fragrant; the slender tube is cylindrical, to 25 mm long, the perianth segments are broad and overlapping, about 25 mm long and usually pure white, and the small, flat corona, about 6 mm long but much wider, is frilled, edged with red and fragrant. 'Actaea' is a cultivar from this division.

Species, *Wild Forms and Wild Hybrids*: All species of wild, or reputedly wild forms and natural hybrids, such as *Narcissus bulbocodium* (Hoop Petticoat Daffodil) and *N. asturiensis* (syn. *N. minimus*), the tiniest of all daffodils, are included.

Split-cupped Narcissi: Usually solitary flowers, each has a cup split for more than half its length. Cultivars include 'Canasta' and 'Soho'.

Miscellaneous Narcissi: The final division includes all *Narcissi* not falling into any of the foregoing divisions. To avoid any confusion of the names of some of the cultivars, the gardener should consult nursery catalogues for both flower descriptions and availability in a particular area.

CULTIVATION Daffodil plants should be grown in sheltered, sunny positions, but many will flower well under the protection of deciduous trees. Although adaptable to most soil conditions, provided that drainage is rapid, *Narcissi* appreciate a clay loam which has been enriched with rotted organic matter and a dressing of complete fertiliser at the rate of 150 g per square metre. Both should be incorporated into the soil several weeks before planting.

Bulbs of *Narcissi* must be planted in a climatically suitable region. Cultivating daffodils in warmer regions is more difficult than in cooler climates because of vigorous, competing weed growth; a thick mulch should be used and recommended planting distances carefully considered. At planting time, soil should be moist, but further artificial watering is not necessary until the leaves emerge.

Depth of planting depends upon bulb size, but is generally 75–100 mm, with distances apart about 150 mm when bulbs are used in ordinary garden beds. A mulch of compost, leaf litter or rotted animal manure should be added after planting. A sharp trowel provides the necessary hole for planting. If soil is known to be poor, each hole should be enlarged so that an enriched section can be provided for the bulb.

Forgetting the exact site where bulbs have been planted is very easy, so labels bearing the bulbs' details and the number and date of plantings should be inserted at the spot. As some *Narcissi* begin to push leaves through the soil very early, ground covers or seasonal annuals can then be planted above them if their exact position is known. *Narcissi* are also ideal for pots and containers. Bulbs can be planted in threes and fives in commercial potting mixtures, providing that a sharp drainage medium such as charcoal is placed in a layer in the bottom of the container. Even bulbs for garden planting can be first placed in containers; when the leaves begin to yellow and die, the containers can be lifted and

moved to an inconspicuous part of the garden to allow the leaves to continue to make food for the bulb.

After emergence, soil should be kept damp and, when flowers appear, weekly applications of liquid fertiliser can be given, strictly in accordance with the directions on the label. When using *Narcissi* for house decoration, the gatherer should cut as long a stem as possible when the flower is in the bud stage. Flowers cut at this time will open in water and last up to a week. After flowering finishes and the leaves begin to lose their green colouring, watering and fertilising should cease.

DAFFODILS

DAFFODIL

Failure to flower or even complete disappearance of bulbs can be traced to insect damage or disease such as flies, maggots and basal rot.

Lifting, division and storage can be done after the foliage has yellowed and died down, indicating that the bulbs are beginning their dormant period. Bulbs should be allowed to remain in one place for two to three years. Division of offsets or flowering-sized bulbs is the customary method of propagation. Offsets can be detached and planted separately until they are large enough to become flowering entities, usually in their second year. Flowering-sized bulbs may be 'double-nosed', with twin flowering points enclosed in the same outer tunic, or 'wall-sided' where the offsets have been removed from the mother bulb. Both types will flower the following winter or early spring, depending on type. After lifting and dividing, bulbs can be stored on trays in a dry cool place until planting time.

Most climatic conditions except hot subtropical and tropical areas are suitable.
PLANTING SEASON: Autumn.
FLOWERING SEASON: Spring.

Nerine

(NERINE, SPIDER LILY, AMARYLLIDACEAE)

This genus of thirty species of graceful, bulbous plants from South Africa bears interesting, spider-like flowers in late summer and autumn before the green strap leaves appear. Flower colours range from white through various shades of pink to deep crimson and scarlet.

N. bowdenii, with sugary pink flowers, grows to about 45 cm. Cultivar 'Blush Beauty' has satin pink flowers; 'Pink Triumph' has larger pink flowers.

N. curvifolia, with scarlet flowers, grows to 45 cm. *N. curvifolia* var. *fothergillii* (syn. *N. 'Fothergilli Major'*) is a vigorous flowerer with bright scarlet blooms spangled with gold.

N. filifolia has more grass-like leaves and pinky red flowers.

N. flexuosa has pale pink flowers and grows to 50 cm. Cultivar 'Alba' has white flowers.

N. humilis, with rose pink flowers, grows to 40 cm. *N. masonorum*, with rose pink flowers with darker stripes, grows to 20 cm. *N. sarniensis*, Guernsey Lily, growing to 40 cm, bears flowers with colours from pink to rose, crimson and scarlet. 'Winter Cheer' has sugary pink flowers in autumn. 'Salmonia' has salmon pink flowers. *N. undulata* has nodding pink flowers and grows to 40 cm.

CULTIVATION Nerines need efficient drainage and a hot sunny position. Propagation is by bulbs which should be planted so that the necks show above the ground during spring, or at the beginning of summer when dormant. Nerines are hardy, but will flower best if undisturbed.

Most climatic conditions except the hot tropics and more temperate higher areas.
PLANTING SEASON: Late summer for summer-dormant types; winter for winter-dormant species.
FLOWERING SEASON: Late summer, autumn.

NERINES X INCHMER

Ornithogalum

(STAR OF BETHLEHEM, CHINCHERINCHEE, ARAB'S EYE, LILIACEAE)

About 150 species of bulbous, herbaceous perennials, native to Africa, Europe and Asia, make up this genus of both hardy and tender plants, featuring slender leaves and attractive, star-shaped flowers that can be white or silvery white and fragrant.

O. arabicum, Star of Bethlehem, Arab's Eye, is a tender species growing to 60 cm with black-centred, white flowers; can be grown in cooler districts if protected from frosts. *O. balansae*, a native of Asia, grows to 5 cm with white flowers striped green. *O. nutans*, a native of southern Europe, is a hardy perennial to 15–35 cm with silvery flowers touched with green. *O. pyrenaicum*, also a hardy native of southern Europe, grows to 90 cm and bears greenish white spring flowers. *O. thyrsoides*, Chincherinchee, a tender species from South Africa, bears exquisite, white flowers in a dense conical spike; makes a choice cut flower. *O. saundersiae*, Giant Chincherinchee, has a head of creamy white summer flowers with a greenish black eye.

CHINCHERINCHEE, *ORNITHOGALUM THYRSOIDES*

O. umbellatum, Star of Bethlehem, growing to 30 cm, has white star-shaped flowers, marked green outside.

CULTIVATION The hardy species grow well in most conditions and soils, in either sun or partial shade. The more tender species can be grown easily in mild conditions, but would need a glasshouse or glassed-in verandah in cold, frosty climates. Propagation is either by seeds or division of offsets.

Wide moisture and temperature climatic range including more temperate high areas and warm areas are suitable, excluding dry inland conditions.

PLANTING SEASON: Autumn, spring for Giant Chincherinchee.

FLOWERING SEASON: Spring.

Oxalis

(OXALIDACEAE)

This genus contains not only ubiquitous weeds but also some attractive ornamentals, including several succulent perennial species. All are South American. The species have characteristic tripartite leaves, which fold up at dark, a caustic sap with a sour taste and the flowers appear in spring or summer. All the weed species have the capacity to produce many bulbils, their main method of propagation. Seeds are expelled from the seed capsule when ripe. Most of the succulent species are deciduous. Check whether Oxalis become weedy in your area.

O. carnosa, a succulent from Chile and Bolivia, growing to 10 cm, has a tuberous root, thick, fleshy stems which become woody and somewhat gnarled, and yellow flowers, three or four together. *O. corniculata*, Creeping Oxalis or Yellow Wood Sorrel, a prostrate weed with creeping stolons, has slender stems and small leaves and the flowers are small and yellow.

O. gigantea, from Chile, a succulent shrub covered in fine hairs and growing to 200 cm with drooping side branches, has oval leaf lobes about 1 cm long and yellow flowers about 2.5 cm across. *O. hirta* is a trailing species with rose pink flowers and will not become a weed. *O. latifolia*, a troublesome garden

ORNITHOGALUM NUTANS

OXALIS MASSONDRUM

OXALIS POLYPHYLLA

Always inspect topdressing and potting mixtures to prevent the introduction of invasive species into your garden. In lawns, creeping oxalis can be controlled with growth regulator type herbicides such as dicamba. In other situations amitrol or glyphosate can be used. Vigorous lawns that are regularly mown can compete satisfactorily.

The climate is not critical.

PLANTING SEASON: Winter.
FLOWERING SEASON: Spring or summer.

weed, has large leaves and pink and purple flowers. *O. pes-caprae*, Soursob, is a plant easily recognisable by its erect habit, yellow flowers and leaves usually marked with small purple spots. Propagating from bulbs and bulbils produced just under the ground, it readily infests gardens and cultivated areas and is a common weed of cereal crops. The similar *O. lobata* is non-rampant and has golden yellow open spring flowers.

O. purpurea, a weed with purple flowers, has dark, round, hairy leaves. *O. succulenta*, a succulent from Chile and Peru, has a short stem, thick branched and scaly, and small, deciduous leaflets on thick, fleshy petioles. The many small, yellow flowers grow on a forked scape.

CULTIVATION The succulents are easy to grow in sandy soil in full sun, and need a dry winter rest. It is wise to grow them in pots in case they become invasive among other plants. Propagation is from seed, or bulbils from the tuberous rooted kind, in spring or summer.

Polianthes

(TUBEROSE, AGAVACEAE)

This genus of half-hardy, herbaceous perennials is native to Mexico and other tropical regions. *Polianthes* have basal leaves, linear to lanceolate, and white or red flowers in racemes. The perianth consists of a long tube and unequal segments, with capsular fruit.

P. geminiflora, growing to 60 cm tall with a globose tuber, has long narrow,

POLIANTHES TUBEROSA

mostly basal leaves to 45 cm. The summer flowers are bright orange-red, in pairs and drooping. *P. tuberosa*, to more than 100 cm, has long, slender leaves often 30 cm in length, and waxy, white flowers that contain an extremely strong perfume; often sold as a cut flower.

CULTIVATION If grown in sheltered sunny positions in well drained, sandy soil, they will withstand a few degrees of freezing temperatures if given winter protection. Plant tubers, with tops just below the surface in spring, in autumn in a sunny, well drained border. Water regularly once first growth appears, then moderately during the growing season; keep soil dry when foliage turns yellow. In cool areas, dig up before the frost begins and store in a dry place during winter; replant in spring. Propagation is otherwise by offsets in the spring. Grow in pots in a rich soil mixture in very frost-prone areas.

Most climatic conditions are suitable. Dry inland and more temperate mountain and tableland areas are also suitable.

PLANTING SEASON: Spring.
FLOWERING SEASON: Summer, autumn.

Polygonatum

(SOLOMON'S SEAL, *LILIACEAE*)

A genus of more than 50 species of hardy, herbaceous perennials, native to many temperate regions of the world. A few species have been cultivated, and these are generally prized for their graceful, leafy stems and white blossoms.

P. biflorum, to 100 cm, has green and white flowers. *P. commutatum*, a native of America, bears large white flowers, and reaches 100 cm in height. *P.* x *hybridum*, Solomon's Seal, small pendant greenish white flowers on arching stems. This is one type frequently grown. *P. latifolium*, to 90 cm, has white flowers with green lobes. *P. multiflorum*, Solomon's Seal, to 60 cm, has hanging tubular white flowers tipped green in leaf axils. 'Flore Pleno' has double flowers and 'Variegatum' has creamy white striped leaves. *P. oppositifolium*, a native of the Himalayas, grows to 100 cm with greenish-white flowers.

CULTIVATION *Polygonatum* thrives in shady positions and needs reasonably rich, well drained soil. Propagation is either by seed or division of the thick rhizome.

Wide moisture and temperature range are suitable, excluding tropical and dry inland climatic conditions.

PLANTING SEASON: Late autumn to winter or early spring.
FLOWERING SEASON: Spring.

POLYGONATUM MULTIFLORUM

Ranunculus

(BUTTERCUP, *RANUNCULACEAE*)

RANUNCULUS ASIATICUS

This large and widespread genus takes its name from the Latin 'rana', a frog, because some species grow well in damp places. It consists of annual and perennial herbs, of which one species, *R. asiaticus*, and its cultivars, are popular bedding plants and excellent cut flowers.

The *Ranunculus* is a tuberous root and very similar in cultural demands to the tuberous-rooted *Anemone*, with which it is sometimes confused. *Ranunculus* have a most unusual-looking storage stem. The tuberous roots appear as small, brown, downward-pointing claws attached to a minute cap. The leaves of the plant are variably dissected and bright green, forming a handsome clump from which the flower stems arise. The flowers of the species are grown for ornamental purposes. *Ranunculus asiaticus* and its hybrids have many more petals than the *Anemone*. The flowers appear above the leaves on thick stalks like bells of satiny crepe paper. The colour range is bright and clear — red, orange, yellow and pink.

R. acris, Meadow Buttercup, from the British Isles and Europe, is a hairy plant with flower stems up to 90 cm long, carrying shining, golden, cup-shaped flowers. *R. anemoneus*, an alpine plant found at Mount Kosciusko, has long-stalked, oval leaves and erect flower stems to 40 cm, bearing several, large, white, many-petalled flowers. *R. asiaticus*, Persian Buttercups, (Garden Ranunculus), is a tuberous perennial with segmented leaves and erect flower stalks carrying large, multi-petalled flowers in late winter and spring. Numerous cultivars are available and can be lifted and replanted each year.

R. collinus, a mat forming Australian alpine, has wedge-shaped leaves and almost stalkless, yellow flowers. *R. lappaceus*, Common or Native Buttercup, is found in Australia and New Zealand, particularly in damp or marshy places. This fibrous-rooted, perennial species has deeply lobed leaves and shining, yellow, cup-shaped flowers.

R. insignis, a New Zealand perennial, has branching rhizomes. The round or kidney-shaped leaves have scalloped margins and the tall flower stems, up to 100 cm in height, carry ten to thirty large, yellow flowers. *R. rivularis*, found in the mainland states of Australia (except Western Australia) and in New Zealand, could include several forms due to the confusion covering the identification of native species. A water loving, mat forming perennial, it spreads to 1 m across with the typical, shining, yellow flowers in summer.

CULTIVATION *R. asiaticus* and its cultivars require a deep, well drained bed in a sunny position that is sheltered from strong wind. The soil should contain plenty of organic matter with, if necessary, a complete fertiliser, about 100 g to the square metre, dug through it some weeks before planting. Plants may be raised from seed sown in seed boxes or a nursery bed in January or February. The seedlings

should be transplanted when they are about 5 cm high, setting them 15–20 cm apart. They should flower in late winter to spring and, at the end of their growing season, will have formed small tubers at the base of each plant. The best of these can be lifted, carefully stored, and set out again the following autumn.

To grow ranunculi from tubers, set claws down, in the bed, 15–20 cm apart and about 5–7.5 cm deep, between February and May. Late planting is the most successful. Unless there is sufficient rain, ranunculi, whether grown from seed or tubers, will need weekly watering and may be given weak liquid fertiliser when the flower buds appear. The tubers are lifted when the foliage has died down and should be stored in a cool, dry, airy place until the following autumn.

Most are water loving, often growing in or near bogs; they are especially suitable for cool climate cultivation. Propagate from cuttings or from root or clump division in spring or autumn and place cuttings in a sharp sand and peat mix of 2:1. Many species also make effective ground cover plants for damp and shady spots.

The climate for Australian and New Zealand species is moist coastal, cool to cold high country; rainfall adequate or better.

Moist temperate and warm climatic conditions are suitable; also milder inland and high areas.

PLANTING SEASON: Autumn.
FLOWERING SEASON: Spring.

Scilla

(SQUILL, *LILIACEAE*)

**SPANISH BLUEBELL,
HYACINTHOIDES
HISPANICA**

From Europe and mainly temperate Africa and Asia, the hundred or so bulbous species that form this genus and bear attractive spikes of single or clustered flowers.

The true English Bluebell (formerly *Scilla non-scripta*) is now classified as *Hyacinthoides non-scripta*. It is the best known of all this group of bulbs and has slim green leaves and nodding, waxy, clear blue bells on sturdy stalks, but it is seen only in cool climate gardens. The English Bluebell is often confused with the Spanish Bluebell (*Hyacinthoides hispanica*, formerly *Scilla campanulata*) which is taller and has larger flowers and is much more adaptable climatically. Like its English relative, it forms large clumps, naturalises rapidly and has some lovely forms in colours of deep blue, pink and white.

The commonly grown squills have varied flower shape and form, some

SCILLA PERUVIANA

with wide-open, star-like flowers, others clustered together loosely in large heads on a common thick stalk, not resembling the flower we think of as a bluebell.

S. bifolia, growing to 15 cm, bears star-shaped, usually blue flowers, though sometimes white or pink, in early spring; suits cool temperate areas such as Tasmania, hill and mountain districts in other states of Australia and the South Island of New Zealand. *S. peruviana*, Cuban Lily or Hyacinth of Peru, growing to 25 cm, has many, deep mauve flowers in a striking dense conical head, from late spring to early summer; prefers warm temperate areas. *S. sibirica*, Siberian Squill, grows to 20 cm and bears a few, attractive, turquoise blue to gentian blue flowers in winter to early spring; cultivars are available. It needs cold conditions. *S. mischtschenkoana* (syn. *S. tubergeniana*), growing to only 10 cm, bears pale blue, almost white flowers, with darker central markings, in late winter to early spring.

S. hyacinthoides has spike-like racemes of soft lilac blue, starry flowers in spring, with, or just before, the dark green broad linear leaves. A Mediterranean plant, it likes a summer and is dormant in autumn to winter.

CULTIVATION These bulbs make striking accents under trees, particularly deciduous ones, or in rock gardens. Easily grown in almost any soil in cool climates, or rich, moist and preferably acidic soil in warmer areas, they will tolerate sun or semi-shade and can be left without lifting for several years. Propagate by bulbs, offsets or seeds. Plant bulbs in autumn at a depth twice their length. If propagating from seed, plants may not flower for up to five years.

Moist coastal and cool to cold high country climatic conditions are suitable, where rainfall is adequate or better.

PLANTING SEASON: Autumn.
FLOWERING SEASON: Winter, spring.

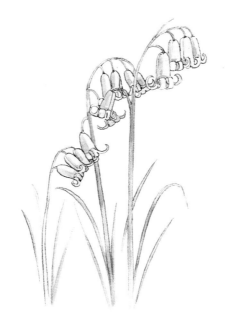

ENGLISH BLUEBELL, HYACINTHOIDES NON-SCRIPTA

Sparaxis

(HARLEQUIN FLOWER, WAND FLOWER, *IRIDACEAE*)

The generic name is derived from the Greek 'sparasso', to tear, and describes the lacerated bracts or spathes. *Sparaxis* is a genus of some six perennial herbs, native to Africa, with cormous roots which develop a basal tuft of linear leaves and erect, branched stems bearing flowers. The flowers are bell-shaped, brilliantly coloured in red, orange, cream, purple and white with contrasting black and yellow centres, and are freely produced in spring.

S. bulbifera, similar to freesias, has narrow, green leaves to 30 cm long and wiry stems. Its funnel-shaped flowers, borne singly at the terminals of branched scapes, are yellow with expanded segments. *S. elegans* (syn. *Strepthanthera elegans*) grows 20 cm high, with broad petalled white or salmon-pink flowers with purple-black basal blotch. *S. grandiflora*, similar to *S. bulbifera*, but larger, with flowering stems to 40 cm, bears three or four flowers on each scape. The blooms vary from deep purple to pink and white, many being given varietal names.

S. pillansi, to 60 cm, has pink flowers with a dark yellow centre, almost white filaments and dark purple anthers. *S. tricolor*, 15–30 cm tall, with green leaves to 30 cm long, bears flowers in spikes on a long scape. The flowers are very showy, ranging from red and pink to orange-red with dark purple base markings and yellow throat, sometimes pale pink and white with purple base and yellow throat. Cultivar 'Alba' has white flowers.

CULTIVATION *Sparaxis* species enjoy a sunny, open position and should be massed together for best effect. Any well drained soil that is not too rich will do, and poor soil can be improved by adding complete fertiliser in early spring. Water well during the flowering season and keep on the dry side at other times.

TESSELAAR BULBS AND FLOWERS

SPARAXIS

The best way to propagate *Sparaxis* is by planting corms, obtained after the foliage dies down in December. The largest corms should be selected, cleaned, dried and stored in a dry, airy place for replanting in February. If not required for propagation, the corms may be left in place for three to four years and will flower abundantly. Fresh, ripe seed may also be planted in December to January to produce seedlings flowering in the following spring.

Most climatic conditions except hot tropics are suitable.

PLANTING SEASON: Autumn.
FLOWERING SEASON: Spring.

Sternbergia

(YELLOW AUTUMN CROCUS, AUTUMN DAFFODIL, *AMARYLLIDACEAE*)

The five to eight species of this genus of bulbous herbs from Europe and South East Asia bear pretty, golden, crocus-like flowers in autumn and grow well both indoors and out.

Sternbergia, Yellow Autumn Crocus, is a small-growing bulb ideal for rock pockets, courtyards or dry banks. The leaves are dark-green, slender straps, appearing with or after the blooms. Flowers are chalice-like with incurved waxy petals of clear yellow on 15 cm stems in autumn.

S. colchiciflora, with stemless, yellow, fragrant flowers, blooms in autumn before the leaves appear. *S. fischerana*, the only spring blooming species, has bright yellow flowers on short stems. *S. lutea*, the most commonly cultivated species, bears bright yellow flowers simultaneously with glossy, linear leaves in late autumn. *S.clusiana* (syn.

S. macrantha) has wider foliage, covered with a light bloom and goblet shaped yellow or greenish yellow flowers.

CULTIVATION Sternbergias are hardy but need a warm, well drained soil before they will produce acceptable flowers. Bulbs should be planted 2.5 cm below soil level. Water well and give plenty of sun in summer. Propagation is by offsets or seed.

Cooler temperate and mild inland and coastal climatic conditions, are suitable; also high areas.

PLANTING SEASON: Summer.
FLOWERING SEASON: Autumn.

STERNBERGIA LUTEA

Triteleia

(STAR VIOLETS, AMARYLLIDACEAE)

Of the 14 species of these cormous herbs, once classified under *Brodiaea*, only one or two are generally cultivated here. They have one, sometimes two, long, linear leaves, wide open flowers borne in clusters on the scapes, and black seeds pitted like peppercorns.

T. grandiflora (syn. *Brodiaea grandiflora*) grows to about 60 cm when in flower and has azure blue to white blooms. *T. grandiflora* var. *howellii* has broader filaments. *T. hyacinthina*, (syn. *Brodiaea lactea*), 20–30 cm, has milky white or mauve puple flowers. *T. Californica*, 60 cm high, has reddish-purple flowers. *T. ixioides* (syn. *Brodiaea ixioides*), Pretty Face or Golden Brodiaea, has a loose umbel of golden flowers with darker purple markings down the centres of the petals, and semi-erect basal leaves. *T. laxa* (syn. *Brodiaea laxa*) is the most widely grown species and the showiest with an umbel of deep to pale purple-blue funnel shaped flowers in spring. Height is 20–30 cm but this plant is variable. 'Queen Fabiola' also widely grown has purple-blue flowers in late spring to early summer.

CULTIVATION Can be cultivated in pots and also make excellent rock garden subjects. Use well drained loam in an open position, planting the bulbs 5–7 cm deep. To propagate, use seed sown in shallow covering of sandy soil or offsets in March or April.

Temperate to warm climatic areas are suitable. Plants can take frost but not below -5˚C.

PLANTING SEASON: Autumn during dormancy.

FLOWERING SEASON: Spring.

Top ◆ **TRITELEIA**

Middle ◆ **ORANGE TRITONIA**

Bottom ◆ **PINK TRITONIA**

Tritonia

(BLAZING STAR, *IRIDACEAE*)

This is a genus of 35 species of herbaceous perennials, native to South Africa and prized for its showy flowers during summer.

T. crocata is a small, flowering plant with leaves that reach 30–40 cm and flowers that are orange-yellow. Hybrids or cultivars are in white, orange and pinks but are seldom sold named. 'Bridesmaid' is white. *T. lineata* has creamy buff flowers with dark veining. *T. rubrolucens*, to 50 cm, has rose coloured flowers. *T. squalida* has flowers tinged with pink and sometimes they are blotched yellow.

CULTIVATION Similar in cultivation to gladioli, tritonias are relatively hardy and can be left in the ground or stored after the foliage has died back.

Moist, cool to warm climatic conditions, excluding hot tropical and cold, high extremes, are suitable.

PLANTING SEASON: Autumn.

FLOWERING SEASON: Spring.

Tulipa

(TULIP, *LILIACEAE*)

The name of this genus of extremely popular, bulbous herbs comes from the Turkish 'tulbend', turban. Tulips had their origin in Europe, western and central Asia and northern Africa, and were first brought to western Europe from Turkey in the mid-16th century. This resulted in so much choice of colour and quality that selection becomes truly bewildering.

Tulips are a true bulb and, except for some of the early flowering types, only suitable for cool climate gardens. They need a precise, low temperature level to mature the bulb for flowering.

The leaves of most varieties are green and thick and generally broadly sword-shaped, often with wavy or undulating margins.

The flowers are usually in the shape of a narrow-mouthed goblet, with thick, artificial-looking, waxy petals, and borne on stout stalks. They are available with wide-open fringed or curving petals, some single, some double. Colours include shades of yellow, orange and red, bizarres (yellow marked with another colour), pink, mauve, cerise, cream and pure white, some candy striped or banded, others streaked. Early and late spring flowering types are offered.

The genus today has many classes, within which the species have been hybridised to such an extent that the classifications made by the Committee for the Registration of Tulips are quite daunting. There are 15 divisions including Single Early and Double Early tulips, and the popular Darwin, Single Late and Parrot classes. In addition, species tulips interest many gardeners and quite a few are available.

The older, still famous cultivar groups such as 'Mendel', 'Old Dutch Mother' and 'Breeder' are now rare and have been overshadowed by Darwin. Such trends in popularity have been governed largely by the suitability of blooms as cut flowers, for which Darwin is the most grown.

Many modern tulips are thought to have had their origin in *T. gesnerana*, which has papery, slightly hairy bulbs, grows to 60 cm tall and has three to five, sword-shaped leaves. Its 7–8 cm long, wide open, cup-shaped flowers are crimson to almost black and the blotches of deep green or black in the floral bases are gold-rimmed. Mostly from *T. gesnerana* have come the common tall late flowering types now grown.

TIM SIMPSON

Above ◆ **'QUEEN OF THE NIGHT'**

Right ◆ **'KING'S BLOOD'**

TIM SIMPSON

MENTON TULIPS

Early flowering include Single Early and Double Early, such as single 'Couleur Cardinal', with cardinal-red flowers, or double 'Peach Blossom' with large deep pink flowers.

Mid-season flowerers, Triumph tulips and Darwin Hybrid tulips (single, excellent for cutting).

Of the late flowerers, there are Greigii Hybrids, Double Late (peony-flowered) tulips and Parrot tulips among others. Darwin tulips are considered among the most useful, as plants have large flowers on long stems for cutting and adapt to many cultural conditions. Cultivars include 'Aotearoa' (large, deep pink flowers), 'Clara Butt' (salmon pink), 'Nadstock Glory' (bright carmine-red, cup-shaped

flowers on tall stems), 'Kansas' (snow white), 'Queen of Night' (semi-open, velvety, maroon to almost black), 'Victor deOlivera' (a red favourite) and 'William Copland' (lilac).

Lily-flowered tulips have single flowers with reflexed, pointed petals forming a delicate star shape and include 'China Pink', soft pink flowers with pure white bases.

Single Late tulips have large, single flowers and are useful for supplying cut flowers and for border planting and include many different colours; 'Burgundy Lace' (heavily fringed, rich rose petals), 'Georgette' (very wide open, yellow blooms edged in pale orange), 'Golden Bronze', 'Inglescombe Yellow', 'Marshal Haig' (almost closed,

crimson flowers), and 'Rosy Wings' (bright apricot pink with white base).

The Parrot types have lacy petals resembling the feathers of parrots in flight and include 'Blue Parrot' (lilac blue), 'Fantasy' (white-etched pink with green-streaked ribs to the petals), 'Firebird' (bright red) and 'Sunshine' (deep golden yellow).

The species themselves are rarer and much sought by collectors; they, too, have been hybridised, and include *T. fosteriana* (short plant to 25 cm with very large, scarlet flowers with black stamens and yellow-edged, black blotches in the base). *T. greigii* (shorter, to 20 cm, with purple-variegated leaves and rich reddish-orange flowers with the same type of black blotches), and

T. kaufmanniana Water Lily Tulip, to 20 cm with star-shaped, open flowers of white, yellow, pink or scarlet with yellow blotches and pink nerves).
T. saxatilis, an open, cup-shaped species, has fragrant lilac-pink flowers with gold centres and spreads quickly; it is known as a 'rock tulip' type.

CULTIVATION Tulips can be grown for massed effect in beds, as borders, in 'natural' clusters in grass, or in containers. For borders and beds, it is wise to keep the colours separated into clumps of twelve to twenty plants. For naturalised plantings, bulbs are best planted when the grass is sown. Tulips will also grow well if planted in amongst protective groundcovers, or will be attractive if mixed with annuals — to give one delightful example: consider planting bright, showy tulips among blue forget-me-nots or white violas.

Unless gardening in a cold climate, it is necessary to lift the bulbs annually, although species tulips can often be left in the ground for two or three years and then lifted to be divided.

When selecting bulbs, choose large, firm, clean and healthy ones or order from a specialist nursery. It must be noted that much tulip stock has a virus made worse by aphids responsible for spreading it in warm, long summers.

For gardeners in mild climate areas, it is recommended to keep bulbs in the crisper of the refrigerator for six to eight weeks before planting.

Tulips do not benefit from early planting: wait until the ground is cooler, between April and May or in late May only for mild areas. Plant the bulbs in full sun where possible, with a cool growing situation. They do not like over-rich soil, but otherwise tolerate a wide range of soils, the absolute essential being perfect drainage; add some lime to acid soils. Dig the ground deeply in advance and add manure or crushed bone meal or blood and bone well before planting. Place the bulbs about 10 cm deep, deeper in light soil or if hotter conditions prevail.

For garden beds, space bulbs 10 cm apart. To grow in a pot, box, or hanging basket (the last for the rock tulip types), be sure the container is very clean before

MENTON TULIPS

TIM SIMPSON

planting, then fill with equal parts of loam, peat and sand or the substitute bulb fibre which must be soaked well first, then squeezed out thoroughly before planting. Bulbs in fibre take slightly longer to flower. Bury the bulbs in the pots under about 15 cm of soil.

Once planted, the bulbs should be watered regularly but sparingly, and indoor, potted bulbs should be watered only in the morning so they can absorb moisture before the temperature drops at night. Watering should be stopped when the leaves brown off and the bulbs should be lifted soon after. Bulbs should be cleaned carefully, dried, then stored in an open-weave bag in a cool,

airy, windless place in a temperature of 15–20°C. Before storing, some people dust their bulbs with napthalene or use some insecticide powder as a protection from moth larvae and other insect infestations.

Apart from aphids and mites, bulbs are subject to tulip 'fire' or *Botrytis*, a fungus leaving a grey cast on foliage and spoiling blooms. Spray early in the season and then before and after flowering with Benlate to prevent the disease.

Most cool climatic conditions, except warm temperate areas to hot tropics, are suitable.

PLANTING SEASON: Autumn.
FLOWERING SEASON: Spring.

Watsonia

(BUGLE LILY, *IRIDACEAE*)

This genus, named after Sir William Watson, a London naturalist and physician of the 18th century, consists of about 40 species of herbaceous, cormous plants with long, tapering leaves and stalkless, colourful flowers borne in gladioli-like spikes. Some species grow to 200 cm in height.

W. *coccinea*, from South Africa, grows to only 30 cm and has blood-red, tubular flowers in summer.

W. *densiflora*, a larger plant, grows up to 90 cm with deep pink flowers, borne on a double-sided spike, in summer.

W. *pyramidata* has rose red flowers and grows to a height of 150 cm or more.

CULTIVATION *Watsonia* species are grown from seeds or corms and prefer a warm, sunny position in rich, well drained soil. Propagation is by seed or by bulbils.

Most climatic conditions, except high areas, are suitable.

PLANTING SEASON: Autumn.
FLOWERING SEASON: Spring.

WATSONIA ROSEA

ZANTEDESCHIA ELLIOTTIANA

Zantedeschia

(ARUM LILY, CALLA LILLY, *ARACEAE*)

The genus name commemorates Francesco Zantedeschi, an Italian botanist and physician who died in 1946. The genus is comprised of eight or nine species of rhizomatous flowering perennial herbs, native to tropical Africa, cultivated for their elegant, usually arrow-shaped leaves and their arum-like flowers.

Z. aethiopica, White Arum Lily, growing to 100 cm, is the commercial 'arum lily', with large white spathes to 25 cm long, surrounding a yellow spadix, flowering in spring. Cultivar 'Green Goddess' has green spathes splashed creamy-white in the centre; 'Childsiana', dwarf, is free flowering. 'Gigantea' is very large. All will grow in garden ponds.

Z. albomaculata, growing to 60 cm, has leaves spotted with white and pale yellow, yellow or occasionally pale pink flowers with purple markings on the inside. Very similar, but without the dark throat, is the yellow *Z. elliottiana*. *Z. rehmanni*, growing to 60 cm, has pale pink to rosy-purple flowers, varying to white with pink edges.

CULTIVATION *Z. aethiopica* thrives in moist situations but grows equally well under average garden conditions. Other species prefer a fairly rich soil and plenty of moisture during the summer months, but watering should be tapered off during their dormant winter period. *Zantedeschia* species are best propagated by suckers removed from the base of the plants in spring or summer. Parent clumps should be divided every three years. Set them again about 12 cm deep with old manure and a sprinkling of fertiliser.

Wide moisture and temperature climatic range, excluding extremes of dry inland and cold high areas.

PLANTING SEASON: Late winter.

FLOWERING SEASON: Summer (*Z. aethiopica* in spring).

Zephyranthes

(FLOWER OF THE WEST WIND, ZEPHYR LILY, WEST WINDFLOWER, STORM LILY, RAIN LILY, *AMARYLLIDACEAE*)

The genus name is derived from the Greek 'zephyr', the west wind, and 'anthos', flower. The genus has over 50 species of attractive bulbous plants with funnel-shaped flowers, related to *Habranthus,* but resembling the Crocus. They come from the tropical parts of America and the West Indies.

The cultivated species, called variously Windflowers or Rain Lilies, are true bulbs which survive being dug up and transplanted in full flower. Transfer from temperate to subtropical regions or vice versa, and increase rapidly in their first season of planting.

The flowers of *Zephyranthes* are similar to those of the Crocus but they are always presented on their sturdy stalks wide open like saucers, with the stamens prominently displayed.

Some have leaves which are glossy green-like rushes, others have leaves narrowly strap-like and distinctively red-tinged at the base. All are displayed with one flower to a stem. Colours are white, glowing pink and golden yellow, depending on the species.

ZEPHYRANTHES GRANDIFLORA

Z. Atamasco, Atamasco Lily, grows to about 30 cm with flowers white flushed with purple in spring. *Z. candida*, with pure white flowers sometimes flushed pink, grows to about 18 cm and is late summer and autumn flowering. *Z. verecunda* is similar to *Z. candida*, with white flowers tinged pink outside. *Z. citrina*, with golden-yellow flowers in summer and autumn, grows to about 25 cm. *Z. grandiflora* (syn. *Z. carinata*), with rose pink flowers in summer, grows to about 30 cm. *Z. rosea*, with rose-pink flowers in summer, grows to only 18 cm but plants sold as *Z. rosea* are usually *Z. grandiflora*.

CULTIVATION *Zephyranthes* species make an effective border display and grow best in warm districts. Before planting, add a thin layer of well rotted organic matter to the hole. It must be thoroughly fragmented so that it will not compact and cause rotting.

Once established, they will thrive without much attention and should normally be undisturbed for a period of about three or four years before lifting for division and replanting. In areas of heavy frost, however, they should be lifted in winter.

They are propagated by offsets set close together in a sunny position. Plant about 7 cm deep in a fairly rich soil, watering freely.

Wide moisture and temperature climatic range, excluding inland extremes, are suitable.

PLANTING SEASON: Autumn, winter to early spring.

FLOWERING SEASON: Late summer, autumn.

Colouring Your Garden All Year Round

TYPE OF BULBOUS PLANT. COLOUR RANGE, HEIGHT	DEPTH X DISTANCE APART
Agapanthus (South African Lily) Tuberous root. Blues, white; single, double; 30–100 cm	10 cm x 60 cm
Allium (onion) Bulb. Blue, purple, lilac, yellow, pink, white; 30–100 cm	5–10 cm x 10 cm
Alstroemeria (Peruvian Lily) Tuberous root. Red, orange, purple, yellow, cream, white; 30–100 cm	12 cm x 30 cm
Amaryllis (Belladonna Lily, Naked Lady) Bulb. Cerise, rose-red, pink, white; 60–75 cm	Neck of bulb above ground level x 45 cm
Anemone (Wind Flower) Tuber. Blue, violet, scarlet, pink, white, lilac, purple, bi-colours; 45 cm	2.5 cm x 15 cm
Babiana (Baboon Flower) Corm. Violet, blues, crimson, pink; 9–30 cm	6 cm x 3 cm
Begonia (Tuberous flower) Tuberous root. Pink, rose, red, orange, yellow, cream, white; 30–60 cm	5 cm x 20 cm
Canna Rhizome. Red, yellow, orange, crimson, pink, white and combinations; 60–200 cm	5 cm x 60 cm
Clivia Tuberous root. Salmon, orange, red; 45 cm	Cover roots, but not crown x 30–45 cm
Colchicum (Autumn Crocus) Bulb. Rosy-purple, lavender, white; 23 cm	Neck at ground level x 15 cm
Convallaria (Lily-of-the-Valley) Creeping rhizome. White, pinks, perfume; 22 cm	2.5 cm x 5 cm
Crinum (Crinum Lily, Veldt Lily) Bulb. White, pale pink; 30–120 cm	Neck of bulb above ground level x 100 cm
Crocosmia Corm. Yellow, orange, red; 100–120 cm	6 cm x 8 cm
Crocus Corm. Blue, sapphire, purple, yellow, orange, white and combinations; 12 cm	5 cm x 7.5 cm
Cyclamen Tuberous root. Pink, purple, salmon, white, red, bi-colours; 23 cm	14 mm x 5 cm
Dahlia Tuberous root. Purple, pink, red, white, yellow, orange, bi-colours, tri-colours in many forms; 45–200 cm	10–20 cm x 60 cm to 100 cm
Dierama (Angel's Fishing Rod, Fairy Fishing Rod, Wand Flower) Corm. Pink, lilac, red, violet; 50–200 cm	7.5 cm x 12 cm

FLOWERING TIME	PLANTING TIME	USES
Summer	Late autumn to early spring	Dry bank, large border, massed display, large tub. Cut flower.
Spring to summer	Autumn	Pots, borders and rockeries.
Spring to early summer	Autumn to winter	Thrive in sunny gardens. Cut flowers.
Summer or autumn	Early spring	Massed display, dry bank, large tub. Cut flower.
Spring	Autumn	Massed display, border edging, rockery, pot and trough. Cut flower.
Spring	Late summer, autumn	Rock pockets, border edging among spring annuals, window box.
Summer	Spring	Trailing varieties good for hanging baskets. Massed bedding. House plants.
Summer to autumn	Winter to early spring	Good for boggy areas. Massed displays.
Late winter to spring	After flowering or in autumn	Naturalises in shady spot, under big trees. Large tub. Cut flower.
Late summer to autumn	Summer	Withstands dry conditions under trees, in rock pocket or window box. House plants.
Late spring	Autumn	Semi-shaded cool spot under trees or shrubs, shady side of shrub border; shallow container. Cut flower.
Summer	Autumn to spring	Withstands dry conditions. Large border, dry bank. Cut flower.
Late summer	Autumn, winter or spring	Hardy plants, grow best in sandy loam. Cut flower.
Late winter, early spring	Late summer, autumn	Naturalise in semi-shade. Cool rockery, at foot of shady bank; trough and pots.
Late winter to early spring	Late summer to autumn	Naturalise in a cool rockery or in shady areas under trees and shrubs. Pots and troughs. House plants.
Summer to autumn	Spring	Bedding plants for massed display, border edging for dwarf types. Cut flower.
Late spring	Late autumn	Rockeries, borders.

TYPE OF BULBOUS PLANT. COLOUR RANGE, HEIGHT	DEPTH X DISTANCE APART
Eucomis (Pineapple Lily) Bulb. Cream, green, purple; 50–200 cm	12 cm x 30 cm
Freesia Corm. Cream, yellow, orange, red, purple, apricot, brown, blue; 45 cm	3–5 cm x 10 cm
Fritillaria Bulb. Yellow, red, orange; 15–100 cm	15 cm x 15 cm
Galanthus (Snowdrop) Bulb. Pure white, white with green; 15–30 cm	5 cm x 5cm
Galtonia (Summer Hyacinth) Bulb. Pure white, sometimes tinged green; 100–150 cm	15 cm x 22 cm
Gladiolus (Sword Lily) Corm. Pink, reds, white, purple, mauve, yellow, copper, bi-colours and tri-colours; 30–100 cm	7.5–15 cm x 15–45 cm
Hemerocallis (Day Lily) Tuberous root. Orange, lemon yellow, pink, purple; 30–100 cm	2 cm x 60 cm
Hippeastrum (Fire Lily) Bulb. Clear reds, pinks, white, bi-colours, some streaked or banded; 30–60 cm	Neck above ground level x 25–30 cm
Hyacinthus (Hyacinth) Bulb. White, yellow, pink, rose, pale blue, deep blue, violet. 15–30 cm	10–15 cm x 15–20 cm
Ipheion (Spring Starflower) Bulb. Blue, white; 30 cm	8 cm x 15 cm
Iris (Bulbous, Rainbow Flower) Bulb. All colours; 12–70 cm	7.5 cm x 15–30 cm
Iris (rhizomatous) Rhizome. Every shade and colour combination and plain colours;30–150 cm	Rhizome half exposed x 60 cm (bearded); 5 cm x 45 cm (beardless)
Ixia (African Corn Lily) Corm. White, cream, yellow, orange, red, pink, blues most with darker base; 30–60 cm	5–8 cm x 5 cm
Kniphofia (Red Hot Poker, Torch Lily) Rhizome. Yellow, red, orange; 60–200 cm	10 cm x 60 cm
Lachenalia (Soldier Boy, Cape Cowslip) Bulb. White, yellow, red, blue, green; 25–40 cm	5 cm x 7.5 cm
Leucojum (Snowflake) Bulb. White with green or pink; 20–30 cm	8 cm x 7.5 cm
Lilium (True Lily) Bulb. All shades, spotted, streaked or banded, some darker colour on reverse petal. 50–200 cm	10–20 cm x 30 cm

FLOWERING TIME	PLANTING TIME	USES
Summer	Autumn, winter to early spring	Attractive features for gardens. Cut flower.
Spring	Autumn	Require little attention. Balcony and window boxes. Cut flower.
Spring	Autumn	Grow well in pots. Borders, rock gardens.
Winter, spring	Autumn	Naturalise in cool shady places; pot plants for bush houses.
Summer	Autumn	Naturalise in dappled shade, middle of herbaceous borders. Cut flower.
Summer	Late winter, spring, summer	Specimen plants in clumps, middle of herbaceous border; smaller species in rock gardens. Pots. Cut flower.
Summer	Autumn to winter	Withstands drought or grows in wet conditions, good bank cover, border, miniatures in rockery.
Late spring	Winter	Hardy and tough for dry areas. Naturalise in sunny spot; large tub. Cut flower.
Spring	Autumn	In drifts in front of border, in cool rock pocket, pots or troughs. Cut flowers.
Late spring	Late summer to early autumn	Beds, borders, rockeries, naturalised plantings or containers.
Spring to summer	Autumn	Extremely versatile. Use in border, rockery as specialty plant. Cut flower.
Spring to summer	After flowering (bearded). Winter (beardless)	Extremely versatile. Most species suitable for hot dry conditions. Cut flower.
Spring	Autumn	Warm border, rock garden, courtyard or house plant. Cut flower.
Summer, autumn, or winter	Spring	Add style to background and border positions, and next to shrubs.
Winter, spring	Autumn	Massed display, borders and rockeries. Pots and baskets. Cut flower.
Autumn, winter, spring	Early summer or autumn (depends on species)	Naturalise in half-shade, pots, banks and edges of water features.
Summer	Autumn to winter	Extremely versatile, some for every corner of the garden in sun or shade; containers. Cut flower.

TYPE OF BULBOUS PLANT. COLOUR RANGE, HEIGHT	DEPTH X DISTANCE APART
Lycoris (Spider Lily) Bulb. Yellow, red, white, pink; 40–60 cm	Neck above ground level x 10 cm
Muscari (Grape Hyacinth) Bulb. Blue, lavender, yellow; 15–30 cm	5 cm x 5 cm
Narcissus (Daffodil, Jonquil) Bulb. Yellow, gold, orange, copper, white, pink, reddish and bi-colours;5–45 cm	7.5 cm–10 cm
Nerine (Guernsey Lily, Nerine, Spider Lily) Bulb. Pink, rose, red, salmon; to 60 cm	Neck at ground level x 15 cm
Ornithogalum (Star of Bethlehem, Chincherinchee, Arab's Eye) Bulb. White with black or green; 5–90 cm	10 cm x 15 cm
Oxalis Tuberous root. Yellow, pink, purple; 10–200 cm	5 cm x 5 cm
Polianthes (Tuberose) Tuberous root. Orange, white, red; 60–100 cm	Top just below ground level x 15 cm
Polygonatum (Solomon's Seal) Rhizome. White; 30–100 cm	Just covered by soil x 25 cm
Ranunculus (Buttercup) Tuberous root. Pink, cerise, red, crimson, orange, bronze; 60–100 cm	5 cm x 15 cm
Scilla (Squill, Bluebell species now in genus *Hyacinthoides*) Bulb. Royal blue, pale blue, white, rose-purple; 15–30 cm	5 cm x 5 cm
Sparaxis (Harlequin Flower, Wand Flower) Corm. Red, orange, cream, purple, white; 20–60 cm	5 cm x 10 cm
Sternbergia (Yellow Autumn Crocus, Autumn Daffodil) Bulb. Yellow; 15 cm	5 cm x 10 cm
Triteleia (Star Violet) Corm. White, azure blue, mauve, purple, gold; to 60 cm	5–7 cm x 10 cm
Tritonia (Blazing Star) Corm. Yellow, orange, pink, red, rose; 60 cm	5 cm x 7.5 cm
Tulipa (Tulip) Bulb. Yellow, orange, red, bizarres, pink, mauve, cerise, cream, pure white, some striped, banded or streaked; 20–60 cm	10–15 cm x 10 cm
Watsonia (Bugle Lily) Corm. Red, pink; 30–200 cm	7.5 cm x 15 cm
Zantedeschia (Arum Lily, Calla Lily) Rhizome. White, yellow, apricot, pink; 45–100 cm	12 cm x 15 cm
Zephyranthes (Flower of the West Wind, Storm Lily, Rain Lily, Zephyr Lily) Bulb. White, pink, gold; 15–30 cm	7 cm x 10 cm

FLOWERING TIME	PLANTING TIME	USES
Late summer to autumn	Summer	Rock pocket, warm bank, courtyard, patio, container.
Spring	Autumn	Massed as garden border, rock gardens, edging beds. Cut flowers.
Spring	Autumn	Naturalises under deciduous trees and shrubs; border, rock pocket, containers. Cut flower.
Late summer, autumn	Late summer or winter (depending on species)	Rock pocket, warm bank, courtyard, container, patio. Cut flower.
Spring	Autumn	Pot plant, garden beds or glasshouse. Cut flower.
Spring to summer	Winter	Rockeries and containers.
Summer, autumn	Spring	Borders and pots. Cut flower.
Late spring	Late autumn to winter or early spring	Under tall tree or in shade of spring-flowering shrubs. Cut flower.
Spring	Autumn	Massed display, border clump, window box or pot. Cut flower.
Winter, spring	Autumn	Naturalise under deciduous tree or shrub, cool rock pocket. Cut flower.
Spring	Autumn	Massed planting. Borders, pots.
Autumn	Summer	Naturalise under deciduous tree or shrub, large rock pocket, paved area.
Spring	Autumn	Pots and rock gardens.
Spring	Autumn	Excellent for massed border effects. Cut flower.
Spring	Autumn	Cool climate, formal bedding display, border edging, pots. Hanging baskets for rock tulips. Cut flower.
Spring	Autumn	Best grown in clumps of about six plants. Cut flower.
Summer	Late winter	Naturalise in open ground, front of shrub border, garden ponds. Cut flower.
Late summer, autumn	Autumn, winter to early spring	Naturalise under shrubs and trees; rock pocket, paved area, courtyard container.

COMMON NAME	SCIENTIFIC NAME	COMMON NAME	SCIENTIFIC NAME
African corn lily	*Ixia* species	lily of the Nile	*Zantedeschia aethiopica*
angel's fishing rod	*Dierama* spp.	lily-of-the-valley	*Convallaria majalis*
angel's tears	*Narcissus triandus*	Madonna lily	*Lilium candidum*
arab's eye	*Ornithogalum* spp.	naked boys	*Colchicum autumnale*
arum lily	*Zantedeschia aethiopica*	naked lady	*Amaryllis belladonna*
autumn crocus	*Colchicum autumnale*	November lily	*Lilium longiflorum*
baboon flower	*Babiana* spp.	Peruvian lily	*Alstroemeria*
beardless iris	*Iris ensata, kaempferi*	pineapple lily	*Eucomis* spp.
belladonna lily	*Amaryllis belladonna*	pink spider lily	*Nerine bowdenii*
blazing star	*Tritonia* spp.	pink tiger lily	*Lilium speciosum*
bluebell	*Hyacinthoides non-scripta*	pink storm lily	*Zephyranthes grandiflora*
	Hyacinthoides spp.	poppy flowered anemone	*Anemone coronaria*
bugle lily	*Watsonia* spp.	rain lily	*Zephyranthes candida*
buttercup	*Ranunculus* spp.	rainbow flower	*Iris* spp.
butterfly iris	*Dietes* or *Moraea* spp.	red hot poker	*Kniphofia* spp.
Californian bearded iris	*Iris douglasiana*	saffron crocus	*Crocus sativus*
calla lily	*Zantedeschia* spp.	Scarborough lily	*Vallota* spp.
Cape cowslip	*Lachenalia* spp.	snowdrop	*Galanthus nivalis*
Causcasian iris	*Iris reticulata*	snowflake	*Leucojum* spp.
chincherinchee	*Ornithogalum* spp.	soldier boy	*Lachenalia* spp.
clivia	*Clivia* spp.	Solomon's seal	*Polygonatum multiflorum*
daffodil	*Narcissus* spp.	South African lily	*Agapanthus* spp.
Darling lily	*Crinum flaccidum*	Spanish bluebell	*Hyacinthoides hispanica*
day lily	*Hemerocallis*	spider lily	*Lycoris* spp., *Nerine* spp.
English bluebell	*Hyacinthoides non-scripta*	spring starflower	*Ipheion* spp.
English snowdrop	*Galanthus nivalis*	squill	*Scilla* spp.
fairy fishing rod	*Dierama* spp.	star of Bethlehem	*Ornithogalum* spp.
fire lily	*Hippeastrum*	star violet	*Triteleia* spp.
flower of the west wind	*Zephyranthes* spp.	storm lily	*Zephyranthes* spp.
Formosan lily	*Lilium formosanum*	summer hyacinth	*Galtonia* spp.
golden calla	*Zantedeschia elliottiana*	swamp lily	*Crinum pedunculatum*
golden rayed lily	*Lilium auratum*	sword lily	*Gladiolus* spp.
golden spider lily	*Lycoris aurea*	tiger lily	*Lilium tigrinum*
grape hyacinth	*Muscari* spp.	torch lily	*Kniphofia* spp.
Guernsey lily	*Nerine sarniensis*	true lily	*Lilium* spp.
harlequin flower	*Sparaxis* spp.	tuberose	*Polianthes* spp.
hoop petticoat daffodil	*Narcissus bulbicodium*	tulip	*Tulipa* spp.
hyacinth	*Hyacinthus* spp.	Turk's cap lily	*Lilium martagon*
Ifafa lily	*Cyrtanthus* spp.	veldt lily	*Lilium* spp.
Jacobean lily	*Sprekelia* spp.	wand flower	*Sparaxis* spp.
Japanese lily	*Lilium speciosum*	wind flower	*Anemone* spp.
Japanese spider lily	*Lycoris radiata*	yellow autumn crocus	*Sternbergia* spp.
Japanese water iris	*Iris ensata, kaempferi*	zephyr lily	*Zephyranthes* spp.
jonquil	*Narcissus jonquilla*		

Directory of Bulb Nurseries in Australia and New Zealand

AUSTRALIA

Broersen Seeds & Bulbs Pty Ltd
365-367 Monbulk Road, Silvan
Victoria 3795
Tel: (03) 737 9202
Fax: (03) 737 9707

Diggers Garden Company Pty Ltd
105 Latrobe Parade, Dromana
Victoria 3936
Tel: (059) 87 1877
Fax: (059) 814298

Drewitt and Sons Bulb Nurseries
Lot 43 Lewis Road, Hoddles Creek
Victoria 3139
(PO Box 212, Woori Yallock 3139)
Tel: (059) 674 307

G. Doyne & Staff Pty Ltd
Lot 1, Ure Road, Gembrook
(PO Box 174, Gembrook)
Victoria 3783
Tel: (059) 681 758

Golden Ray Gardens
Lilium Nursery
1 Monash Avenue, Olinda
Victoria 3788
Tel: (03) 751 1395

Mary Van Graas
The Blue Dandenongs Bulb Farm
PO Box 3
Monbulk
Victoria 3793
Tel: (03) 756 6766

Tesselaar's Padua Bulb Nurseries
357 Monbulk Road, Silvan
Victoria 3795
Tel: (03) 737 9305
Fax: (03) 737 9743

Viburnum Gardens
8 Sunnybridge Road, Arcadia
New South Wales 2159
Tel: (02) 653 2259
Fax: (02) 653 1840

Windyhill Flowers Pty Ltd
Macclesfield Road, Monbulk
(PO Box 183, Monbulk)
Victoria 3793
Tel: (03) 756 6669
Fax: (03) 752 0243

NEW ZEALAND

Beautiful Begonias, (G&R
Hardwick)
Rockland Rd, Clifton, Takaka
South Island
Tel: (03) 525 9058

Blue Mountain Gardens, Tapanui
West Otago
South Island
(No telephone)

Daffodil Acre, (Bill van Djik)
PO Box 834, Tauranga
North Island
Tel: (07) 552 5383

Dunhampton Lily Fields, (JH &
PM Millchamp)
1 RD, Ashburton
South Island
Tel: (03) 303 9743

Ferry Road Dahlias
29 Ferry Rd, Martinborough
North Island
(No telephone)

Joy Plants, (Lindsay Hatch)
Runciman Rd, RD2 Pukekohe
North Island
Tel: (09) 238 9129

Kereru Nursery, (C Challenger)
Okuti Valley, Little River,
Canterbury
South Island
Tel: (03) 325 1086

Parr's Daffodils
Junction State Highway 16 & 18
Kumeu, RD 2
North Island
Tel: (09) 412 8566

Parva Plants (1987) Ltd, (Ian
Duncalf)
PO Box 2503, Tauranga
North Island
Tel: (07) 552 4902

Chris Duval Smith
Kalaua via Pokeno,
State Highway 2
North Island
Tel: (09) 233 5818